MW00533933

Carl,
Thanks for being
such a great
supporter of President
Trump. Let's keep
winning!
All my best,
Paul S.

Robert Scott Kiger

FROM POVERTY TO POLO TO POLITICS

A LIFE LEADING TO TRUMP

Robert Scott Kiger

Copyright © 2018 Robert S. Kiger

All rights reserved. No part of this publication may be reproduced, distributed, or transmitted in any form or by any means, including photocopying, recording, or other electronic or mechanical methods, without the prior written permission of the publisher, except in the case of brief quotations embodied in critical reviews and certain other noncommercial uses permitted by copyright law. For permission requests, write to the publisher, addressed "Attention: Permissions Coordinator," at the address below.

ISBN-13: 978-0692118597 (Robert Scott Kiger)

ISBN-10: 0692118594

Printed by Amazon, in the United States of America.

First printing edition 2018.

Publisher
339 Cocoanut Row.
Palm Beach, FL 33480

www.RestoringUSA.org
© 2018 Robert Scott Kiger

U.S. $28.95 | CANADA $36.95

DEDICATION

To my loving parents, Dick and Maxine
To Scott Devon, Marty Vanier, and
Virgil Lovell

To my brothers and sisters:
Marjorie Roslund, Terry Moore, Richard Kiger
James Kiger, and especially Donald Kiger

To President Donald J. Trump for
Making America Great Again!

**Without your support and guidance,
my life and this book would not be
possible.**

CONTENTS

DEDICATION

THE SERIAL ENTREPRENEUR

From Poverty to Polo to Politics

A Life Leading to Trump

CONTENTS

Robert Scott Kiger

ACKNOWLEDGMENTS

Special thanks to my friends for always having my back:

Leland Badger, Doug Hanson, Stanley Tate, Ron Allen, Tom Burke, Kent Stevinson, Derek Smith, Steve Crowder, Ned Remington, Connie and John Wise, Scott Swerdlin, Terry Cotton, Chuck Correll, Ken Baker, Brooks Thornhill, Dr. Richard Saladino, Sylvan Corazzi, Mario Paniccia, and Peter Radloff.

Thank you, Samantha Elphick, for your amazing editing advice and expertise.

I will forever be grateful!

i

Preface

Walking by the floor to ceiling windows of my 17th Street, Denver loft, I stop short. Right before my eyes, I'm astonished by the beauty and nobility of *The Beast* passing by on the street below. I swallow hard realizing that it is *Cadillac One* and the 40-car motorcade carrying President William Jefferson Clinton. Staring in wonder, I watch in disbelief. I can only speculate what it must be like to be part of this amazing entourage...

That was 1997. Today, as I step into a black SUV to meet *Air Force One* on the tarmac at the Palm Beach International Airport, I'm filled with honor beyond belief to be driving with the motorcade of President Donald Trump. With a smile on my face, I reach up to touch my lapel pin, my security pass which allows access for today's drive from PBI to Mar-a-Lago.

My Secret Service Flag Lapel Pin has become one of my most treasured possessions. Now, as I pull up to the majestic *Airforce One*, I think back and wonder how it was possible for me to get here. I never in my wildest dreams thought that a poor kid from Okemos, Michigan would have one of the greatest privileges in the world. You may question how I got here?

Here is a look at my life journey
From Poverty to Polo to Politics.

ii

Chapter One

THE EARLY YEARS

Sitting in my cottage in the heart of the opulence of Palm Beach, Florida, it's difficult to think back to the early years of growing up in poverty during the late fifties, and the hard tasks that would lie ahead. Two loving parents ameliorated my situation, along with five supporting brothers and sisters. Because our house was in great disrepair, I think many suspected that the shack we grew up in was abandoned. My mother, father, and five siblings shared a twelve by fourteen-foot cabin. I was the youngest of six children and I am sure that it was easier for me since I didn't know what being poor in Okemos, Michigan represented.

My father quit school when he was in the eighth grade to work on my grandfather's farm. I'm not sure when or where he got the training, but he was regarded as a master carpenter. I would watch him agonize for days on end over a lathe to make a new spindle leg for a chair. Dad never knew how to charge customers for his hard work, he was way too gracious, and that got to be a problem. Consequently, he would work on a single chair for several days' and only made a small pittance.

Our little cabin was split into two rooms and a hallway. The hallway contained a small refrigerator and a sink, which had a hand crank for getting water. My three brothers and two

The Original Kiger Estate

sisters slept on four bunk beds in one room, while my mother and father, with me between them, and my little sister using a chair for her bed, slept in the other room. When I recall our sleeping arrangements I smile knowing how romantically delightful that must have been for my parents.

Our cabin had no indoor plumbing, and trekking to the outhouse in the middle of a Michigan winter wasn't fun. For me as a four-year-old, it wasn't terribly traumatic, but for my brothers; Dick twelve, Don fourteen, and Jim fifteen, along with my sisters; Marge eight and Terry ten, this had to be tough. The old shack was built on very shallow ground, making it extremely prone to flooding. One night during an exceptionally strong rain storm

Dick & Maxine Kiger on their honeymoon in 1948

the cabin flooded, the water had risen to two feet deep. I remember standing on my parent's bed so that I wouldn't get wet. The rainstorm got to be the last straw for my father and shortly thereafter; we moved to a new house that seemed like a mansion at the time. It was a three-bedroom home with one bathroom. The 1600-sq ft. home cost $16,000. It had indoor hot and cold running water, a toilet, and even a shower! What a step up. My sisters had a bedroom that they shared, and my three older brothers also shared a room. I bunked in with my sisters. Finally, my parents had some much-needed privacy.

However, we hadn't escaped poverty. We still had to get food from government agencies. You haven't lived until you have tasted powered milk mixed with tap water. Every week my mother could get two pounds of lard, cartons of dried milk, rice, flour, beans and bread from the federal agencies. I can remember at Christmastime being able to go to the local firehouse and receive a toy from the firemen. What great heroes they were in the eyes of this young boy.

We were living in an area surrounded by folks with money. The house was situated across from Michigan State University. Most of the children that I went to school with were sons and daughters of doctors, lawyers and MSU professors. They loved razzing the only poor kid in the school and were relentless, poking fun of my clothes and mocking the fact that I had only one pair of shoes. I didn't have too many friends in school, but by the time I was eight-years-old, I was working every day after school and on weekends.

Two grad students at Michigan State, Gary Minish, and Harlan Richie had prize Hereford steers that needed grooming to show at the State Fair, and the famous Chicago International. I worked daily for them, grooming and exercising their prize livestock. They turned out to be my first great mentors. When we showed the steers at the Michigan State Fair, I felt proud that

__Robert Kiger Exhibiting the Neil Orth Steer at the 1969 Chicago International__

I had contributed to a job well done!

There wasn't enough money for hotel rooms, so we slept on the straw in the barn, next to the prize livestock. Gary and Harlan were successful; they went home with Grand Champion Steer honors. This was a big deal, as the Grand Champion got auctioned off for big money.

I earned a reputation for hard work, like my dad, which paid off. After graduation, Gary and Harlan gave my name to two other grad students who also had steers to train and groom for competition. Larry Cotton and Neal Orth hired me to help with their cattle.

I had been working for them several years when Neal took me to Seaton, Illinois to work on the family farm in the summer of 1968. We showed cattle at the Iowa and Illinois State Fairs, as well as the Chicago International. Still, with no budget for a hotel room, we slept in the barn! After I returned home, I met a man who influenced me beyond my comprehension.

His name was Professor Byron Good. He oversaw all the University Farms at Michigan State University. Notably, Dr. Good turned out to be the greatest animal scientist of his time.

One day, right out of the blue, he made me an offer. "If you come over to my farm and work every day after school, I will give you a lamb to train and show at the county fair," he offered. *WOW! My very own animal to show,* I thought. While I was relishing in the prospect of such an offer he kept speaking, "I will teach you how to clip, groom and train the animal for competition, and after you show the lamb at the county fair, it will be auctioned off, and you can give me back my original cost and you keep the rest for your college education," he suggested.

I was flabbergasted! "W-why are you doing this? No one has ever told me that I should go to c-college b-before!" I stuttered. The Professor, deviating from his usual mastery of language, looked at me very sternly and said, "If you are ever going to amount to a hell-of-beans you must get a college education," he spoke

Dr. Byron Good
Michigan State University

adamantly. I was caught off guard because my father hadn't even graduated from high school, and now Dr. Good was suggesting I should go to college? I accepted the generous offer and was prepared to do whatever it took. Throughout my time with Professor Good, a great sense of self-assurance, confidence, and discipline got instilled in me.

After diligently clipping, grooming, and training the animal for months to ready my lamb for competition, I eventually showed my protégé and to my surprise, the "wether" lamb won its class and then he was sold at the fair's livestock auction. What I didn't anticipate was how attached I had become to my lamb. I watched him grow from birth to a class champion, and I didn't want to let him go. After the auction, I took him back to the fair barn. I sat in the pen hugging him and cried my eyes out knowing my lamb would soon be sent to slaughter. I received the money from the auction and paid Dr. Good for his original cost. With the balance of the funds, I suddenly had more money than I had ever seen in my life.

I will never forget these great men, all of whom became famous in their own field of study; they helped shape my early work life. To Dr. Gary Minish, Dr. Harlan Ritchie, Neal Orth, Larry Cotton, and most of all Dr. Byron Good, I owe these men a great deal.

I didn't have a High School social life; my friends were college students and graduate students. College parties were much more fun than the high school parties, probably because I never got invited to high school parties. In the summer of 1970, Terry Cotton, Larry's brother, came to visit from

Deadwood, South Dakota. We became great friends, and our friendship continues to this day. During that summer, Terry had to haul a horse to Deadwood and asked if I would ride along to keep him awake for the 17-hour drive. I accepted thinking it would be great fun to spend some time with my best friend, meet his parents and take in the sites of historic Deadwood.

About halfway through the trip, Terry looked tired, he leaned over and dead seriously he told me, "I need you to drive."

"What? I shouted, "I'm only fifteen, I have no driver's license, and never driven a truck with a horse trailer tagging along," I protested.

"Really?" he questioned sarcastically. "That's unfortunate, but it's damn time you learned," Terry spouted. "Look, it's two in the morning and there aren't too many cars on the Interstate. All you have to do is keep it at 65mph, drive straight, and keep between the lines."

He pulled over and I reluctantly got behind the wheel. Up until then, I had only driven a truck out in the middle of a horse pasture. Thoughts were whirling through my head... *What if I wreck, what if I get stopped with no driver's license...will I go to jail?*? Four hours later, to my great relief, Terry woke up and offered to get behind the wheel once more. I could now stop crapping my pants; I had made it without causing any harm to anyone or the horse tagging behind us.

———————————————

Chapter Two

THE RODEO TEAM

Deadwood is a city rich in "Gold Rush" and "Old West" history. Mount Moriah Cemetery has the graves of Wild West figures like Wild Bill Hickok and Calamity Jane. This historic town is filled with old cowboy saloons that still look like Wyatt Earp could walk in at any minute.

Back in those days, the Deadwood bars served 3/2 beer and, if you kind of looked eighteen-years-old there were no questions asked or any need for identification, you were served with no trouble. Therefore, Terry and I had a lot of fun in the cowboy saloons. *The Days of 76 Rodeo and Parade* were worth the trip to Deadwood. The parade got held on Friday and Saturday and it's the favorite parade that Deadwood has all year. The Parade is often an hour long, and features many horses, historic wagons, and carriages.

Something I will never forget was the day when we got to ride on an old stagecoach in that famous event. To be able to ride on a stagecoach that was probably seventy-years-old was an astounding experience. It was exciting to think who might have sat in that seat in the 1880's.

Annual Days of 76 Parade Deadwood, SD

But, in the evening things got a little crazy when the Hell's Angels converged on Deadwood. Those bikers and cowboys didn't mix too well. The city would have the MP's from Ellsworth Airforce Base come to Deadwood to keep the peace. Still, fights would break out, but the MP's always won. During this time, Terry was celebrating his High School Graduation and I got to go to the big party that his graduating class held on top of Mount Roosevelt. They built bonfires that were huge and seemingly out of control. I couldn't believe they didn't burn the mountain down. They must have known what they were doing because the next morning all the trees on Mount Roosevelt, along with the four Presidents etched into nearby Mount Rushmore, were still standing.

During our trip, I fell in love with my first girlfriend. To this day, I am not sure that my lifelong friend Terry Cotton realized that it was his sister. She was a year older than I, but when you're fifteen and sixteen, it doesn't matter. Consequently, I headed back to Michigan. Unfortunately, the love that I found in Deadwood didn't last, given that we were 1,200 miles and five states apart.

After seeing my first Pro Rodeo in Deadwood, I immediately fell in love with the sport and ached to learn how to participate. Terry was an accomplished roper and had a great roping horse, but I didn't have the money for a horse, so roping was out of the question. I then decided to learn to ride bulls and bareback horses. I entered rodeo school to learn the sport of rodeo.

After the bull and bareback riding school, we entered the rodeos on the weekends in Michigan. I am not sure what loophole the Michigan State University Rodeo Team had to jump through, but they allowed me to be a competing member of the MSU team, even though I was still in High School.

Robert Kiger competes at M.S.U. Rodeo in 1970

My mother went crazy when I would get stomped into the mud. I can still hear her screaming from the stands. I never got badly hurt, just stepped on by the horses and knocked around by the bulls. I had many more broken bones and injuries from my later participation when I took up Polo.

We traveled to an Intercollegiate Rodeo at Wisconsin State University. Jeff, one of our teammates, was a bull rider. He was damn good despite his big disadvantage; he was legally blind. Jeff's corrected vision was 20/400. His glasses were a quarter inch thick and resembled prescription ashtrays. His vision was so impaired that when he rode bulls we would sit on the bucking chutes and scream at him, to let him know what direction he should run when he got bucked off. During the Wisconsin Rodeo performance, Jeff was sitting with us on the bucking chutes after he had ridden. The chutes were about eight feet high. One of the other riders had just finished his successful 8-second ride and was walking back in front of the chutes.

Now, when this cowboy from Wisconsin got in front of us, Jeff didn't see him, and unknowingly, jumped off the chute and landed on top of his shoulders. They both hit the dirt hard. The Wisconsin cowboy got pissed off causing a fight to break out in front of the entire audience. He didn't understand that our friend Jeff couldn't see him. We immediately pulled Jeff out of the scuffle without too much mayhem. It wasn't Jeff's fault, and it ended up that they both got fined for fighting in the arena during the performance.

I never was very good at the sport of rodeo, and I always joked that my best event was the after party!

Robert Kiger and the entire MSU Rodeo Team

At the age of seventeen, all my friends were college students from the rodeo team, including my girlfriend who was a barrel racer on the team. She was teased about robbing the cradle... I was seventeen and she was twenty-one. My father had one rule, you can stay out at night, but you better get your ass out of bed and be in school at 8 a.m. every day. After a long night of partying with my barrel racing girlfriend and the rest of the rodeo team, I rolled in at two in the morning. My dad met me at the door, and the only thing he said to me was "You know you can get in a lot of trouble after midnight?" he quipped.

Getting in that late, 7 a.m. came around very early, and in accordance with my father's rule, I left the house for school at 7:30 a.m. with a massive hangover. On my way out the door, I grabbed a sleeping bag. I knew I would never stay awake during class so I drove to the nearest rest stop on the Interstate, crawled into the back seat of the car and went to sleep in the sleeping bag. At 1 p.m. I woke up, it was about 100 degrees in the car, and I was drenched in a pool of sweat with a massive headache. My father was right, nothing good happens after midnight!

After graduation, Dr. Byron Good and Larry Cotton offered me a job at the Michigan State University Beef Cattle Research Center. This was my first big job! I didn't have enough money for college, so the plan was to work for a couple of years and save enough money to attend. At that time MSU bred some of the world's most sought-after prize Angus breeding stock. MSU provided me with a huge house to live in and a truck to drive. I had made it! Professor Good oversaw of all the University Farms. He would constantly test my knowledge, driving out to the farm every day he would bombard me with questions:

"How many cows are in this field, Kiger?"
"How many calves?"
"How many are female?"
"How many males?"
"How many of the cows are pregnant?"
"What are the sires of the calves?"

Of course, he knew all the answers to the questions that he would deliver in rapid succession. I knew that I had better get the answers right, or tell him I didn't know. If I tried to fake it or guess, he would know I was full of shit, and I would be in big trouble with him.

Upper Rt: Dr. Ron Nelson,
Chairman MSU Animal Science Dept.
Lower Rt.: Me, next to my dog Judd, and the rest of the crew
at the MSU Beef Cattle Teaching Center

This was a brilliant man that you couldn't bullshit. He

called the purebred livestock at MSU "Living Art". Dr. Good reminded me of General Patton. Even during winter months in Michigan when it was 10 degrees out, he would ride a horse every morning at 5 a.m., then dress in his suit and tie and head to his office on campus. He was a great horseman and a great mentor.

My first taste of how politics can be a nasty business came to me one summer day at the MSU farm. I was out in the middle of a pasture working on a fence. A black sedan drove out to the middle of the field where I was working. Two men in suits got out and came over to me, introduced themselves, and told me they were from the local union. They looked like Abbot and Costello. "We would like to welcome you to our union," they said in unison.

They continued to inform me that I was working seven days a week, sometimes ten to twelve hours a day. They told me that I wasn't being paid over time, and I wasn't making enough money. "When you become a member of our union," the skinny one added, "we can stop all of this, and get you the compensation that you deserve." They then told me that the union dues were only $52.00 per month and they could deduct it right out of my check. "I am happy with my current compensation and work schedule," I told them. They continued to insist that I was being overworked and underpaid. It came time for me to tell them a thing or two.

"You see that truck over there?" I pointed, "Well I get to use it for free." I decided to proceed. "I don't even have to buy the gas! And did you notice the big white house on the road when you drove in from campus? Well, that house is mine for free! I don't even have to pay for the phone or the electricity. Furthermore, at the ripe old age of eighteen, I'm making more money than my father, who has worked like a dog all his life, not me," I said shaking my head from side to side. I told them aggressively, "I couldn't be happier."

"Let me put it to you this way young man, either you sign this membership form now and join our union, or we will have this job that you seem to cherish so much, terminated by this afternoon," the gruff fat guy told me.

I told them they could get back in their car and leave. I was not going to be a member of their f…ing union.

As they drove away, I suddenly was stuck in panic mode. I immediately headed back to the barn office to call the great mentor, Professor Good. After I told him the situation, he laughed.

"Don't worry. I'll handle it," he reassured me.

By the next morning, my job title was changed from Assistant Herdsman to Lab Technician, which was a non-union position. Ever since then I have had great disdain for labor unions.

Chapter Three

COLLEGE DAYS

I married Renee Raines at the age of nineteen, way too young. She was an excellent horsewoman and a beautiful person inside and out. Being a workaholic, our honeymoon wasn't exactly a woman's dream. Both of us drove a load of cattle, that MSU had sold, to an Angus breeder in South Dakota.

Reflecting back, she should have left me right then. Can you imagine riding in a truck for 17-hours and then staying at the Holiday Inn in Aberdeen South Dakota, freezing cold in the middle of the winter for a honeymoon? What a patient girl she was, and what an ass I must have been! Renee and I lived in the big MSU house, but divorced just after two short years. I now regret losing this great girl, and I blame the breakup on my young age and immaturity.

Life went on, I had saved enough money for one year of college tuition. I wanted to become a Veterinarian. The Ph.D.'s in the Animal Science Department at Michigan State all received their doctorate degrees at Kansas State University. KSU had a great Vet School, so they convinced me to attend Kansas State. After paying the tuition, there wasn't much money left for me to go off to school. Nevertheless, I loaded up the back of my truck and headed south with everything I owned to start a new chapter. I had enough gas money to get there and about $200.00 left over for food.

I hadn't organized a place to stay, so when I rolled into Manhattan, Kansas, not knowing what the hell I would do, I decided to stop at "Kites", a local watering hole next to the campus. I sat at the bar ordered a burger and a 3/2 Coors beer. I introduced myself to two other students sitting next to me, David Cheves and Carman Trevitt. It turned out that they were both members of the K-State football team. I told them of my dilemma; I had no money and nowhere to live.

David was quick to respond, "We're living in the football dorm, you could come over to the dorm and sleep on the floor in our room," he suggested. Carmen grinned in agreement. Feeling relieved, I took them up on their offer. After living there for three months, I was surprised that no one had ever realized that I wasn't a member of the team. Like all football players, I ate like a king for free in the dorm cafeteria, choosing steak and eggs in the morning, and steak almost every night.

David was a quarter Cherokee Indian from Pawhuska, Oklahoma. As a kicker on the special teams squad, he had a great football career ahead of him. Carman, who weighed about 300 lbs., and played center for the team. I remember how interesting it was to watch Carman eat; he could consume two dozen donuts in one sitting. All David wanted to do is rope steers in the rodeo. I constantly tried to tell him to focus on his football career. Finally, I suggested, "When you go pro you can buy your own arena and rope all the steers you want." But, unfortunately, he didn't listen. He was always getting in trouble for being late for practice or not showing up at all.

One evening David, Carman, and I headed to the bar for some fun. David started to drink hard booze. I didn't drink anything and was completely sober. But David was determined to get inebriated. We stayed for about two hours and David decided we needed to go to another party. Carmen remained at the bar and David and I left for the party. The Indian in David and the hard liquor wasn't a good mix. It propagated the crazy in him, and when he left the bar, he was driving at an insane rate of speed. God must have been looking after me because for some reason seeing the campus approaching I quickly blurted out.

"David, I need to s-stop by the dorm and pick up a jacket," I said, not recognizing the fear in my voice.

"You have to be kidding, right?" he asked annoyed, but pulled into the parking lot and let me out.

I went straight to the dorm room and sat on the bed feeling paralyzed. Something prevented me from going back down to the truck where David was waiting. I stayed in the room until I finally heard him leave without me. I let out a sigh of relief.

I learned the next day that his crazy ill-fated driving through campus continued that night. The police had witnessed his erratic driving and attempted to pull him over. David wasn't about to stop for anyone. The police chased him through town doing 70 mph in 30 mph zones. When they reached the outer edge of town David failed to negotiate a turn, lost control of the truck and drove head-on into a big oak tree.

The crash put him through the windshield. Now I know that if I were in the passenger seat, being sober, I most likely would have died in the crash. I still thank God for that one. They say that drunk people survive car accidents because they are so relaxed. Luckily, David survived the crash. I visited him in the hospital the next morning. His face was cut up, with broken bones to his face and arm. That got to be the last straw for the KSU football coaches. He got kicked off the team, lost his football scholarship, and had to leave school.

When David left school, I moved out of the football dorm and moved into a trailer positioned on a ranch outside of Manhattan. I worked on the ranch breaking steers. It was a good thing that I was young because I got kicked, punched, gored, stomped, and dragged on the ground by these mean as hell Brahma-Angus steers. To get through college, I worked the ranch job as well as another job on campus and survived with the help of student loans.

My first real taste of entrepreneurialism came in the winter of 1977. I was a college junior and got selected to be the chairman of the Block & Bridle Horse Show. The National Block & Bridle Club is designed to promote a higher scholastic standard and a complete understanding of animal science among student members and to enhance the professionalism of students who will one day be leaders in the agricultural animal industry.

The club didn't have much of a budget to put on the show that year. I convinced them to allow me to invite other colleges and universities to K-State to compete in the horse show. This would obviously bring in more entry fees and more revenue to the club. Previously, the spectator admission to the horse show was $2.00, and the attendance from the community was always dismal.

I needed to find a way to bring more people in and raise the price of admission. Weber arena, where the horse show got held, would hold about 2,000 people. In previous years, the horse show would have 100 or 200 people show up for each performance of the two-day show. Consequently, they would raise $1,000 to $1,500. Not good enough!

The horse show had the usual equine performance classes as well as calf roping and barrel racing. If I was going to get more people to attend and raise the price of admission, I needed a big draw.

I met Ray Simms, who was known as one of America's greatest auctioneers of purebred cattle and horses. His second cousin was Leroy Van Dyke. Van Dyke had many number one country music hits in the mid to late 60's. He had recorded more than 500 songs, dozens of them making the charts. His hit song *Walk On By,* which he recorded in 1961, was named by Billboard magazine in 1994 as the biggest country single of all time based on sales, plays, and weeks on the charts.

It stayed number one on the U.S. country chart for nineteen weeks. He may have been one of the first cross-over artists since this single reached number five on the Pop charts. It sold more than 1.5 million copies. But the song that Leroy Van Dyke got most noted for was *The Auctioneer.* He was inspired by his cousin Ray Simms whose story is told in this song. This single topped the Pop Music Charts and sold more than 2.5 million copies. I now had my draw for a bigger crowd and more revenue. Did I really think that I could get this country music star to perform at our little show, with no money to pay him up front? I figured that all he could say was no.

I called Ray and asked him for Leroy's number. I quickly called Van Dyke and told him that we were raising money for the Block & Bridle Club and I would like him to perform three performances. He informed me that his standard fee was $30,000. I was lost for words until finally, I admitted.

"There is no way we could pay that much, but thank you for taking my call," I politely told him and went to hang up. He stopped me.

"Wait a minute . . . Hmmm," He began. "If possible, I would like to help out the Animal Science students," he said and went on to explain why. "I graduated from the University of Missouri with a degree in agricultural journalism, and obviously, I had a great love for the agricultural industry, the students, and livestock."

I listened intently and felt my adrenaline soaring. *Is this happening?* I thought, and then his voice broke through, "How about rather than my normal $30,000 per performance fee, I give you a deal?"

KSU BLOCK & BRIDLE
HORSE SHOW
Weber Hall **Manhattan**
Feb. 11- 12
Fri., Feb. 11, at 7 p.m. Sat., Feb. 12, at 12 Noon
Saturday, Feb. 12 at 7 p.m.
Tickets Available At Lee's Western Wear, Manhattan
Or Phone 913-532-6131
Or Write
Block & Bridle Club, Weber Hall, Manhattan 66506

"W-what do you propose?" I asked with a lump in my throat, my excitement rising.

"What if I were to charge you $15,000 for all three performances, and you can pay me after the three shows get done?" He stated.

"Absolutely, we would be most grateful, thank you . . . thank you!" I answered after I had finished falling off my chair.

As soon as I hung up the phone I thought, *What the hell have I just done! I have obligated the club for $15,000 for an event that usually generates $1,500 at most.*

Now, I had some real selling to do! Not only to the club members but also the faculty advisors. I formulated a plan and asked for a meeting. Once everyone was present, I told them what we had got offered. Nervously, yet convincingly, I put forth my sales pitch.

"If we raise the admission price to $5.00, we just need to sell 3,000 tickets to break-even after we pay Van Dyke his fee," I began, looking at their blank stares and quickly continued, "I know 3,000 tickets looks like a huge stretch, given we usually only sell 600 tickets for all three performances, but I feel this is a sure thing given the popularity of Leroy Van Dyke!" I concluded. After many questions, as to the viability of this proposal, they reluctantly agreed.

Robert Kiger and Leroy Van Dyke after The Show

Show day came and we ended up selling out all three performances. The gross was $30,000; we paid Van Dyke his $15,000 and put $15,000 in the club treasury. The generosity of Leroy Van Dyke will always hold a big place in my heart. Not to mention how he had saved my ass.

Chapter Four

WHY IT'S EASY TO LOVE AMERICA

To become a vet, you first get a four-year undergraduate degree, and then one must complete four years of vet school. I finished a four-year B.S. Degree in three years by taking on more than a full load each semester and attending summer school. I received my degree in Animal Science in June 1978, I was so burnt out from the school schedule, I needed a break, and decided to go to work for a while.

I took a job that Larry Cotton and Harlan Ritchie, mentors from my days at MSU, had recommended me for. The ranch was south of Buenos Aires, Argentina in the small town of Nueve de Julio. Argentina in 1978 was very politically unstable. The country had suffered a military coup only two years prior, and now a murderous military junta ruled. I was wondering what the hell I had gotten myself into when I stepped off the plane and was marched through customs by military men with AK-47's. Driving through BA on the way to the ranch there were soldiers on every street corner with guns on their hips, and AK-47's on their shoulder.

My job on the ranch was to train and groom Angus show cattle for the big competition coming up in Palermo. The owner of the farm was a wealthy Argentine race car driver, who had purchased and imported the Angus show cattle from Michigan State University. Not a sole on the ranch spoke a word of English. I didn't speak Spanish but very quickly learned a sufficient amount to get by, especially how to order food! It makes you a little crazy to not be able to have a conversation with anyone for months on end.

After three months on the ranch, I had the cattle ready for the big livestock show in Palermo. At the same time, the FIFA World Cup Soccer was taking place. Argentina won the World Cup that year defeating Netherlands 3-1. The Dutch claimed Argentina cheated, so to add insult to injury, the night after the final match someone blew out the front of the Holland bank across the street from the Intercontinental Hotel where I was staying. The blast was so loud, I jumped from the bed in the middle of the night, and I thought for sure that war had broken out. Including me, no one was hurt in the bombing. I went back to sleep, and woke up early the next morning for the big show.

The cattle that I had been training won top honors at the show, Grand Champion Bull, and the Grand Champion female. I was paid $3,000.00 for my four months of work. When it was time to get paid the owner took me to the bank to get U.S. dollars. The Peso was so discounted at the time, he brought two suitcases full of Pesos to the bank to exchange for $3,000 U.S.

My time in Argentina proved to be a great experience, and it taught me one thing, there is no better place than America. The simple things that we take for granted daily, like a phone system that works, medical services, an honest police force, etc., just weren't available in South America, no matter how much money you might have.

It was time to go back to the U.S., and when I stepped off the plane in Miami, I truly wanted to kiss the ground. I was convinced then, and still maintain today, that America is the greatest nation on the earth. Despite all the problems you might see promulgated every day on Cable News, America is second to none and is easy to love.

Chapter Five

ANGUS ASSOCIATION TO ARMAND HAMMER

The American Angus Association, St. Joseph, Missouri, is the largest purebred breed association in the world, and they needed a regional manager in the northeastern sector of the United States. So, after returning to the U.S., I was offered the position. My territory was all the New England states, New York, Pennsylvania, New Jersey, Maryland, Delaware, and Virginia. I decided to live in historic Rhinebeck New York, fifty minutes north of New York City. This is a beautiful part of upstate New York, and during that time the region was consumed with some of the most elaborate Angus cattle farms in the country.

I met some incredibly wealthy business people throughout my travels with the Angus Association. Many New York businessmen were in the Angus Cattle business for the lucrative tax advantages and incentives that were available at the time. One such man was Jerome Brody, who owned Gallagher's Steakhouse, the Four Seasons, the Rainbow Room, and the Oyster Bar in Grand Central Terminal in New York City. When you went to an Angus Cattle sale at Mr. Brody's farm, he served everyone dinner before the sale. The staff at Gallagher's Steakhouse presented the most elaborate dinner fit for a king. Mr. Brody is no longer living, but if you visit Gallagher Steakhouse in New York City, you will see photographs of his prize Angus livestock hanging on the wall.

Many other notable individuals had Angus farms in my territory, and since I was with the association, they all were very welcoming to me. I spent a lot of time with Rachel Breck of the Vanderbilt family. Rachel owned a beautiful Angus cattle farm in Connecticut. She was one of the most gracious ladies I have ever met. I would spend hours with her as she told me stories of big band leader Bennie Goodman, President Harry S. Truman, and Bing Crosby. It surprised me the amount of interest that came from celebrities, comedians, and political members who were fellow Angus owners in my territory and close friends of Rachel.

I continually met other famous people who had farms in my territory. I remember my delight when I visited Hildene Farm in Vermont. It was a bolt-from-the-blue when I learned Mary E. Beckwith, the founder of Hildene Angus, was the granddaughter of President Abraham Lincoln.

There was a long list of CEO's and Senators from upstate New York and Connecticut. My client list also reached wealthy individuals in Virginia and Massachusetts, all with a passion and interest for cattle investments. I could go on and on with the ostentatiously rich and powerful people that I had the privilege to work with. I was star struck by these captains of industry, politics, entertainment and even sports.

After a short six-month stay in New York, the association purchased the Angus Journal from a private individual. They asked me to return to St. Joseph, Missouri to serve as an Advertising Manager for the monthly publication. At first, I was disappointed to be leaving my territory and all the interesting people, but taking on the magazine management exposed me to a whole new perspective of the Association.

The National magazine gave full dedication to the

promotion of the Angus breed. We produced a magazine consisting of 200 to 250-pages each month. Now, I fully understood the pressures of running a magazine and what publishing people go through every month. It was like your life starts over every thirty days.

In 1979 there was no such thing as desktop computers. News copy was typed into a special typeset machine that printed out a sheet of copy. Then the copy got individually cut and pasted onto a large photo board. After pasting copy and photos onto the board, the board would be shot with a large camera to produce a negative that then got sent to the printer. The magazine business in 1979 was a much more arduous, time-consuming, labor and employee intensive business.

While I was at the Angus Association headquarters, I met a lovely girl who also worked at the association. Our relationship grew and she eventually became my second wife. This too would later prove to be a bad decision that led to another matrimonial failure.

My First Cover Photo of the Ken & Dianne Conway Kids.
shot at the R&J Ranch, Briggs, Texas.

During my travels in the Northeast as Regional Manager, I had met a wealthy gentleman by the name of Virgil Lovell. His brilliance for business was evident and always intrigued me. He asked me to join his Lovana Farms operation as Executive Vice President. Virgil was only one year older than me, but I could learn a lot from this man. He was the only person that I had ever met who had an actual photographic memory. Whatever Virgil read, he could regurgitate it verbatim years later.

Lovana Farms was located in the small southern town of Clarkesville, Georgia, eighty miles north of Atlanta. I moved to Clarkesville and assumed my new position as Executive Vice President. My wife didn't like Clarkesville, nor did she want to leave her job in Kansas City and live in Georgia. Consequently, my second marriage became a disaster, and I found myself divorced for the second time.

Lovana had fifty employees that I was to supervise. However, it wasn't long before I realized I was not second in command to Virgil Lovell. His father Carlos, and his uncle Fred Lovell, were very much involved. At best, on a good day, I was fourth in command. I didn't mind this as Carlos and Fred were great cattlemen and I could absorb an enormous amount of knowledge from them. Virgil, Carlos, and Fred were the largest landowners in North Georgia and possibly in the entire state of Georgia.

Notably, Carlos and Fred made and ran moonshine from the early 1900's to the early 1960's. Carlos told me that one of his biggest customers was old man Joe Kennedy!

"When the money went out of the moonshine business," Carlos told me, "I think Fred and I were the only moonshiners in eight counties that didn't turn to hard drugs!" I got to sample the 180-proof moonshine just once! Believe me, it could knock your socks off!

Robert Kiger with Virgil Lovell, and Sale Manager Burke at a Lovana Production Sale

Virgil had purchased some of the country's finest Angus breeding stock and Lovana Farms took its place on the map as one of the nation's top breeding facilities. Production sales were held on the farm in the spring and fall. Record prices were paid for Lovana Angus by investors and top breeders from the U.S. and Argentina. There were big tax incentives at the time for passive investors to own breeding partnerships. Virgil was a genius putting these partnerships together.

I had always been a big fan of Liberty University's founder, Dr. Jerry Falwell. In 1956, at the ripe old age of twenty-two, he started the Thomas Road Baptist Church in Lynchburg, VA. He began the *"Old Time Gospel Hour"* which got nationally syndicated on radio and television. I always watched the Sunday TV show and thought he was the most remarkable public speaker I had ever heard. In 1967 Dr. Falwell founded Liberty University in Lynchburg and by 1979 he was a major force for conservative political activism. He rallied and registered millions of his Christian supporters to back Ronald Reagan for President through his *"Moral Majority"* lobbying group.

I came up with an idea to promote both Lovana Angus and help Dr. Falwell. I proposed to Virgil and Carlos that they donate five Angus breeding females to Liberty University. We would keep the females at Lovana Farms, breed them to the top bulls, sell the calves, and donate all the profits to Liberty University. They liked my idea and agreed!

I made a phone call to the University and conveyed my idea to Dr. Falwell's administrative assistant. I was told someone would get back to me. I nervously waited for two weeks and finally, the word came back, Dr. Falwell agreed to the plan and would like to visit the farm. He had an advance team much like President Trump has today. I was impressed! This guy is busier and more important than I thought.

Many people at the time thought that Dr. Falwell and many other televangelists were not sincere and were only in it for the money. I too had my doubts. This was quickly ameliorated when Dr. Falwell made his visit to the farm. We picked him up at a Habersham County Airport, a private facility not far from Clarkesville. The agenda was down to the minute and we were instructed not to deviate from that schedule, because after leaving the farm, Dr. Falwell would head to DC to meet and have dinner with Republican officials on the election of Ronald Reagan.

When Falwell's Gulfstream Jet landed, I was impressed, to say the least. As he stood in the doorway of the jet, I was surprised, I had never seen a private jet that you could stand straight up in. When Falwell stepped off the plane, we were waiting on the tarmac to whisk him off to the farm. However, he didn't come right over to us. Instead, he immediately walked over to a group of school children that happened to be visiting the airport on a school field trip.

Robert Kiger and Dr. Falwell inspect the "Liberty Angus" females.

He knelt to their level greeting them with his huge smile as he handed out *Jesus First* pins. Here was a man who kept a crazy "Presidential-like" schedule who just took twenty minutes to greet and hug twenty elementary students. I saw first-hand his devotion and commitment to his faith. I knew right then and there his sincerity was real. This was a man consumed with the dissemination of the "Word of God."

Lt-Rt. Virgil Lovell, Robert Kiger & Dr. Falwell Holding the Angus Bull that His New Females will be bred to.

We arrived at the farm, and enjoyed a wonderful lunch, before going out to inspect Liberty University's donated

Angus stock. Dr. Falwell was very impressed with the quality of the females that the Lovell's had donated, and "The Liberty Angus Breeding Herd" was born!

Virgil Lovell did a lot of investment business with Financial Service Corporation (FSC) in Atlanta. The firm handled the private placements that he developed for livestock investments. I wanted to move back to the big city. Consequently, I decided to move to Atlanta and work for FSC. They sent me to the Investment Training Institute in Atlanta to obtain my Series 7 License, which would allow me to sell private placements and other investment instruments.

FSC had approximately 650 financial planners scattered throughout the country. One of my responsibilities at FSC was to give overviews of the FSC Private Placements to the financial planners that would come to the Atlanta headquarters from time to time. The Private Placements involved a multitude of industries. As the teacher, I learned a lot about real estate, movies, record deals, livestock, oil and gas, and other investments that got packaged in Private Placement offerings with major tax savings and write-offs that were available to investors.

Hugh Bowman was my main mentor at FSC. Hugh had a broad client base that was mostly made up of doctors and Delta Airline pilots. It was his responsibility to train me to become a Financial Planner. I would put together a personal financial plan and then together we presented the financial plan to the client. After listening to Hugh make several presentations to a half dozen different clients, he decided it was time for me to step up to the plate.

So, one early evening we drove to the residence of a Delta pilot. As we stepped out of the car, he sprung it on me that I would give the presentation. I freaked out, but when we got to sit down I began to explain the program to the Delta pilot and his wife. Unbeknownst to me, I had a bad habit of finishing my sentences with. . . *YOU KNOW.*

About two minutes into my presentation I made a statement about the program and at the end of the sentence, I added my tag. Suddenly, Hugh looked at and piped up.

"No I don't know!" he shouted.

I felt the blood rise in my face. *Hugh what the hell are you doing! I am always polite and quiet during your presentations.* I thought. I continued with my speech and after making another declarative statement, I tagged it again with *YOU KNOW.*

Right on cue, Hugh piped up and shouted: "No, I don't know!" His mocking of me went on most of the night. We finally finished and got back into the car, I looked over at him.

"Hugh, what the heck were you doing and why in the hell did you embarrass me in front of the clients?" I asked.

"Do you know how irritating it is to hear you end almost every sentence with, *YOU KNOW*? he answered

I said, "I really do that?" Hugh assured me that was exactly what I was doing, and informed me that he only piped up about one-third of the time. I was saying this after almost every sentence.

Although it was painful, my mentor, Hugh Bowman just taught me a very valuable life lesson. That experience broke me of an exasperating habit in one evening. Until this day, I occasionally catch myself saying *YOU KNOW* and I immediately think back to Hugh Bowman and remind myself that it's an extremely obnoxious habit.

Growing up I was never exposed to racism or bigotry from my parents or anyone in my circle of friends and family. I knew that there were people out there who were racist regarding blacks, but I had no knowledge of people being anti-semitic.

FSC was holding an annual dinner at one of the elaborate private country clubs in Atlanta. This dinner was for executive staff members. I went inside the beautiful club and joined the cocktail hour. I looked around the room and asked one of the other FSC executives.

"Where is Goldberg and Johnson and Brownstein and Coleman?" My friend looked at me as if I had come from outer space.

"Kiger, don't you know anything! They don't allow Blacks and Jews in this club." I was shocked! I knew there was discrimination against Blacks, especially in the South, but I had no idea that anyone discriminated against Jews. I couldn't understand this bigotry. It was like the Civil War had been fought last week! Feeling dismayed, I wondered why FSC would hold an event that excluded certain staff. At the ripe old age of twenty-eight, I discovered that it wasn't just the poor kids who faced humiliation and disparagement.

While at FSC, I heard that Dr. Armand Hammer, Occidental Petroleum, was looking for someone to put together some investment packages and do marketing out of their Denver office. Occidental was the largest independent oil company in the world. The need presented a great opportunity for me. I made some calls and landed a job with Occidental Petroleum. I became the marketing director in Oxy's agri-business division . . . Dr. Hammer's pet project. He owned OXY Arabians, and Iowa Beef Processors, which was the largest meatpacking plant in the country. He also owned Ankony Angus, the largest purebred Angus herd in the U.S., and an animal genetics center outside of Denver, CO. My office would be at the OXY genetics center.

I left Atlanta in September 1982 and headed west. The day I left Atlanta it was 82 degrees. When I arrived in Denver on September 8th, it was 28 degrees and snowing. My mind was trying to figure out what the hell I had got myself into. I thought that I had left the Michigan cold for good.

What I didn't know was that it was common for it to be 30 degrees and snowing one day and sunny and 75 degrees the next. If you like four seasons, there is no better place to live than Denver.

One of the fun perks of being a part of Dr. Hammer's pet projects was going to the Angus cattle and Arabian horse events with him. Several times I traveled to the headquarter office in Los Angeles. In the spring of 1982, I was called to Dr. Hammer's office for a meeting. His office was like something I had never seen before. Austere and laden with power - plush carpet, dark mahogany wood walls, a fireplace, and a massive leather-topped desk. The desk and the walls were adorned with photographs of Dr. Hammer with Richard Nixon, Gerald Ford, Ronald Reagan, Hollywood Stars, and numerous world leaders.

Dr. Hammer was a great conservative and a big backer of Richard Nixon, Ronald Reagan, and the Republican Party. Hammer contributed $54,000 to Richard Nixon's 1972 re-election Presidential campaign. This donation would lead Hammer to plead guilty to three misdemeanor charges for what Government prosecutors deemed illegal. Hammer insisted that he did not know that he had broken the law. To hopefully stay anonymous, the contribution was made using names of friends of Tim Babcock the former Governor of Montana. Dr. Hammer was fined and placed on probation for one year.

In August 1989, President George H. W. Bush granted Hammer a pardon. Dr. Hammer told the press, "I deeply appreciate President Bush's action in clearing my name. Having spent my lifetime fighting injustice, this vindication reinforces my abiding faith in the American system of justice."

When I was shown into Dr. Hammer office, he was on the phone with a U.S. Senator. He motioned me to sit down in front of his desk, while I listened to one side of the conversation. He was talking to the Senator like he was a junkyard dog. Dr. Hammer continued to scold him. Then I heard, "No Senator, no one is listening, no one taps my phone. If you tap my phone, you go to jail!" The political power that he possessed was unimaginable.

Oxy Arabians were some of the most elite bred stallions

Another Great Mentor: Industrialist, and Entrepreneur
Dr. Armand Hammer

and mares in the world. When Dr. Hammer got into the Arabian horse business, he soon discovered that the best Arabians in the world were in communist Poland. The problem was the Soviet Union would not allow export of the horses. This didn't stop Hammer. He knew that the USSR had a chronic meat shortage throughout the country. Hammer worked out the perfect deal with the USSR Deputy Prime Minister, Leonid Kostandov. He would supply the Soviet Union with packaged beef from his recently acquired Iowa

Beef Processors, and in turn, he would purchase and export two of the world's top Arabian stallions; El Paso and Pesniar to California.

Arabian horse auction sales were like Hollywood productions. The spotlights went up, the curtains opened, machine-made fog blew across the stage, and the sale of the magnificent mares and stallions would begin. Each one of the production sale owners would try to outdo the other. Wayne Newton's sale in Las Vegas had to be more extravagant than the production sale of film director Mike Nichols, and so on.

Attending an Arabian sale in Scottsdale, Az with Dr. Hammer, turned out to be a star-studded event. Captains of Industry and Hollywood mavens were in the crowd and the National Media cameras were in full force. They panned to close-ups of Charleton Heston and Wayne Newton while being interviewed. Warren Beatty and David Murdoc of Dole Pineapple were acknowledged. The greatest moment of all was when the cameras followed the presenter's voice calling:

"Over here, quick over here! Isn't that Oxy Petroleum's Dr. Armand Hammer?" The sale began, they were too late.

The auction sale went off smoothly with lots of money and studs changing hands.

After the sale, ABC interviewed Dr. Hammer and asked, "Dr. Hammer, what intrigues you about Arabian horses, and why do you like the Arabian horse business?" The young reporter asked.

"I bought El Paso and paid one million dollars for him, and purchased Pesniar for one an a half million. Now, it looks like this year I will sell about $15 million in stud shares in Pesniar and about $10 million in stud fees for El Paso. I think that it is easy to see why I like the Arabian Horse Business, wouldn't you say, young man?"

Chapter Six

THE SERIAL ENTREPRENEUR

KIGER & ASSOCIATES

In the fall of 1982, I traveled with Hammer to a Lasma Arabian sale in Kentucky, where I met the Executive Chairman Steven Markel and Alan Kirshner. They happened to be the principal men of the Markel Insurance Company in Richmond, VA. Markel insured all the Oxy Arabians for Dr. Hammer and most of the other significant breeders in the Arabian horse business.

Markel earned reverence as the premier Specialty Lines insurance broker who insured the horses for mortality. One can imagine that if you buy a horse for a million dollars, you would want to have your horse protected for the trailer ride home, and a few years after, at least until you got some money back on your investment. During a conversation with

Steven Markel, I informed him of the expensive Angus cattle getting sold privately, and at auction all over the country.

Some Bulls were selling for a million dollars for half interest and females selling for $250,000 to $750,000. Furthermore, only one company in the U.S. had 100% of the entire cattle mortality insurance market. The company was American Livestock.

I convinced Markel that with my contacts in the Angus business, I could take a major portion of the market away from American Livestock. We agreed that I would open a divisional office for them in Denver. When I got back to Denver, I resigned from Oxy and went on the search for office space. I settled on the 17th Street Plaza in the heart of Denver's business district.

In the fall of 1983, my father passed away after a brief fight with lung cancer. He was a Navy Veteran during the Second World War. He worked in the shipbuilding yards where they insulated the ships haul with asbestos-laden materials. Like many other World War II Vets, he was a smoker for most of his life. Those two contributing factors took their toll. But, the saddest fact was my father had worked like a dog all his life. Then at the age of sixty-five, he decided to retire. Six months later he was dead. I resolved right then I would never retire. Some people, especially men, lose their purpose and zest for life after retirement.

W. Richard Kiger

My father was a great man who I can honestly say never cheated anyone out of a dime. He was a man of few words and never gossiped or talked disparagingly of others. His example always reminded me and likened the advice of my favorite author F. Scott Fitzgerald, who wrote in my favorite book "The Great Gatsby".

"In my younger and more vulnerable years, my father gave me some advice that I've been turning over in my mind ever since. Whenever you feel like criticizing anyone, he

told me, just remember that all the people in this world haven't had the advantages that you've had."

I opened the Markel divisional Office in the spring of 1984. My friend Tom Burke was the founder of the *American Angus Hall of Fame* and owned the nation's premier *Angus Sale Management Company*. Usually, Tom controlled whether the prize Angus breeding stock would be insured after they got sold at auction. The only problem, there was only one company that was insuring cattle. American Livestock, headquartered in Chicago Illinois, had a monopoly on the business. I was now the alternative.

The current rate to insure cattle at the time was 5% of the animal's value per year. I proposed to Tom that I would lower the percentage to 4.5% for his clients. He wasn't a big fan of American Livestock, so it became relatively easy to sell the proposal. Tom helped me promote my company to his clients, and the Denver Markel office took off. I traveled to all the major sales in the country and would intentionally sit next to the sale clerk. Then at the end of the auction, I got to sign the new buyers up for the animal mortality insurance on the spot. American Livestock was furious; they had never experienced this new thing called competition! Thanks to Tom Burke, I managed to build a significant book of business in an incredibly short time.

In the summer of 1984, I took the leap for the third time. I married Robin Dreschel. Robin was a Flight Attendant for Frontier Airlines and later for Continental. The flight benefits for a spouse were significant at the time. I was always flying somewhere in the country, three to four times per week. I could walk up to a designated counter for airline employees, and buy a ticket to anywhere in the country for $25. The benefit to me was a considerable expense saving for my company. Instead of spending $2,000 per week on airfares, I was spending $100.

Robin and I honeymooned in Cancun Mexico. The first day on the beach, I began swimming alone and body surfing on the high waves that were present that day. About thirty yards from the beach I put my feet down to start walking back, suddenly there was no bottom, I felt the undertow sweeping me out even further. Being a good swimmer my attempts continued, but I was no match for the powerful current. Each time I thought I had swum back far enough, I tried to stand up on the ocean floor, again there was no bottom, and fear began flooding through me. I had never experienced anything like this, and I knew I was in big trouble. I started yelling for help and I could see people on the beach watching me, including Robin and our friends, but no one was coming. I quickly became exhausted. I couldn't fight any longer, and no help was on the way. A calming feeling came over me; I gave up and passed out.

I wish I could tell you that I saw a big shining light and angels singing, but the next thing I remember was a big crowd standing around me. There I was, lying flat out on the sand with a Mexican kid kneeling over me pumping my chest, while I was puking up salt water. I obviously didn't know anything about undertow. I felt embarrassed to be in that situation, however, the Mexican kid tried to console me.

"Don't worry, you are the 15th person that I have saved in the past two weeks, and three of them died!" He blurted out without thinking. S-*shit you could have been the fourth to die!* That thought raced through my mind. I tried to give the lad some money for saving my life and he retorted, "No thanks, I work for the hotel, and it's my job to watch out for folks. He said confidently."

Wow! What an incredible young man. Walking around the hotel for the next few days, people would stop me and ask, "Hey! Aren't you that guy who almost drowned yesterday?"

There weren't any signs or warning flags on the beach alerting the public of the imminent danger. After we returned to the U.S., I found an article in the New York Times reporting on the large number of U.S. Citizens who had drowned in Mexico during the past two months, all due to the undertow, and the lack of appropriate cautionary signs. So, I guess I was not the only victim. I always wondered if this was a bad omen for my brand new marriage.

In 1985, I convinced Markel to let me buy out the *Book of Business* that I had started for them. Stephen Markel acted incredibly generous, giving me a million-dollar *Book of Business* for pennies. Thus, Kiger & Associates got established.

JNB Exploration occupied the office suite next to Kiger & Associates. I met a young fellow named, Neil, who seemed in charge of the office. I later learned that Neil was the President of this oil and gas company. He had two partners that were well-known Colorado real estate moguls, Bill Waters and Ken Good. Bill Walters was known as the Donald Trump of Denver. I became curious as to why there always seemed to be security people outside the door of JNB exploration. Stupid me! I finally realized that the Neil that I got introduced to was Neil Bush, the son of the Vice President of the United States George HW Bush.

Good and Walters had invested vast sums of money in JNB Exploration. Bush started the company with $100 of his own money. He received $10,000 from Good, $150,000 from Waters, and low and behold a whopping $1.75 million credit line from a bank that Waters controlled. During the next few years, Good would plunk down another $3 million to JNB.

In 1985 Bush became a director at Silverado Savings and Loan. While on the board, Bush helped to approve loans to Waters and Good. Good was approved for a $900,000 line of credit and an $18 million loan modification from Silverado.

But, with tumbling oil prices and other economic downturns in Denver, Silverado collapsed in 1988.

When the Federal Deposit Insurance Corporation stepped in, the proverbial *shit hit the fan.* Bush was up to his ears in a conflict of interest problems and lack of his fiduciary responsibilities regarding the loans to Good and Waters. Now, there is nothing inherently wrong with conducting business with people that you know or whom you are friends with, but Bush failed to disclose his relationship with Good or Walters. For instance, the $900,000 that Good borrowed from Silverado got used to finance an Argentina oil venture, whereby Bush was a partner.

By December 1988, the FDIC closed Silverado and subsequently filed a $200 million lawsuit against Bush and other directors and officers of Silverado. According to Douglas Jones, the Senior Deputy Council for the FDIC, *"Silverado was the victim of sophisticated schemes and abuses by insiders, and of gross negligence by its directors and outside professionals."* The scandal received national attention. As the Washington Post put it, Neil Bush was now the poster child for the S&L Scandal. Conveniently for daddy

Bush, the FDIC shut-down of Silverado was delayed from October to December, so that it would be after the 1988 Presidential election. Walters defaulted on $106 million in loans, and Good's loan default left Silverado holding the bag for $32 million. The Silverado failure would eventually cost taxpayers $1.6 billion. The total S&L collapse in the U.S. evinced a $1.4 trillion price tag. At that time, it was one-quarter of the U.S. National Debt!

Neil wasn't the only "Bush" entangled in the S&L debacle. Brother Jeb defaulted on a $4.5 million loan used to finance an office building in Broward County, Florida. Regulators appraised the building for $500,000, leaving taxpayers with the $4 million deficit. Neil Bush escaped a criminal charge, and the FDIC civil suit against Bush got settled for a meager $50,000.

I continued to work hard to build the Kiger & Associates insurance brokerage, but I felt compelled to further my education. The University of Denver had a great MBA program. My friend Bill Daniels was a big supporter of DU. Bill was a wealthy businessman in Denver. He was known as the Godfather of the cable industry, and he convinced me that

DU is where I needed to go. He had made substantial donations to the university, and later his philanthropy included a $22 million gift to DU.

After his death in March 2000, the business school got renamed the Daniels College of Business. I wasn't sure if I could tackle an MBA degree and run my insurance business, but I had to try. Fax machines and computers were not in mainstream business use. I was still using a Telex machine to communicate with Lloyd's of London in my insurance office. But, since the launch of the Commodore 64 home computer in 1982, it was becoming evident that PC's were going to play a prominent

Robert Kiger Receives MBA Finance from the University of Denver

part of everyday business and home use. I knew nothing about computers. The MBA degree would force me to learn, as almost all academic work I would do in the MBA program would get done on a computer.

In June 1987, I graduated from the University of Denver with an MBA in Finance. Even with a new degree under my belt, all was not rosy. I had other problems. My third marriage was headed for the toilet. I identified with my old pal Bill Daniels - he had been married four times, so I asked him if he was going to get married again?

"NO, after the fourth marriage I figured I wasn't very good at it!" his response was adamant. The collapse of my third marriage didn't set me back. I picked up and dusted myself off.

I had been watching a beautiful new building going up across the street from the office that I currently occupied. The Tabor Center was magnificent. I knew that I wanted a space in that tower! I ended up being the fifth tenant to sign a lease in the new Tabor Center. I moved into space on the 23rd floor and found that almost the entire balance of the floor was occupied by KBPI, KNUS. They were AM/FM stations.

I met Ken Hamblin who was a nationally syndicated AM political commentator on KNUS. Ken was ultra-liberal, and he knew that I was a die-hard conservative. Known as "The Black Avenger" on the *Ken Hamblin Show*, he was definitely on the wrong side of the aisle for me. Nevertheless, we became great friends. Ken would stop by my office almost daily for a testy political debate. One afternoon, while listening to Ken's show, I heard him make a promise to his listeners,

"If Gary Hart becomes the Democratic nominee for President; I am joining the Republican Party."

I couldn't believe my ears, so I immediately got up from my chair, grabbed an autographed photo of George H.W. Bush, a Republican Presidential Task Force lapel pin, and a voter change of party registration form. Laughing to myself and trying to keep a straight face, I walked down the hall and into the studio. I peeked through the window at him and he waved me in while he was on the air.

I sat down and he introduced me as Robert Kiger his arch-conservative combatant.

"How are you my friend?" he asked. I bent closer to the microphone, I wanted his audience to be sure to hear what I had to say.

"Ken, I want to be the first to welcome you to the Republican Party. Congratulations!" I reached out to shake his hand. "I want to award you with a signed Bush photo, a Republican Task Force pin, and a voter registration change form," I told him and placed the materials on his desk. Well, I wish it had been captured on TV. I will never forget the look on his face.

Due to his extramarital affair with Donna Rice, Gary Hart never became the Democratic Nominee. But Ken later turned out to be a right-wing conservative; A complete 180 turn in his thinking. He became known as the black Rush Limbaugh. I would like to think I had something to do with his change of heart. In his book "Pick a Better Country," Ken wrote to me the following...

"To my dear friend Robert, you were right all along."

By the early nineties, Kiger & Associates was growing at a rapid pace and earnings were up. Then an unexpected setback hit, an IRS audit. Jack Wade wrote in his book *Confessions of an IRS Agent... "The IRS has unique powers over Americans that the CIA, NSA, FBI, and local police can only dream about."*

I believe that all American's should pay their fair share and the IRS should go after abusers. But, I soon learned why so many people hate the IRS. After their first request for documents, they camped out in my office for almost a year. Every two weeks they would bring in a new and long laundry list of requested documents. They were in my office so frequently, I decided to give them a designated office with a desk. As they always do, the audit was not only for the current year, but the three previous years as well.

They took up so much of me and my staffs time, it got to be a big problem, preventing us from concentrating our efforts on business. It seemed like we were working for them instead of making money.

After twelve months of dredging through my books, their final finding was I hadn't paid myself enough salary. I had paid myself $34,000 in 1987, and they said that someone with my education and experience should be paid at least $60,000. To get them off my back, they wanted me to cut myself a check for $30,000, and pay back Federal Income and Employee Taxes on that amount, along with penalties and interest.

I refused, 1987 was my first year in business, and this request was ridiculous. Furthermore, I didn't have an extra $30,000 laying around in the corporate account to write myself a check. That resulted in going to court. I thought this would get dragged out even longer, but to my surprise on that first day, after the judge reviewed the case, he looked up and announced loudly.

"IRS why are we in here? IRS, you are way out of line!" Then the judge turned to me. "Mr. Kiger, I am sorry for the waste of your time. This case is dismissed!"

Now that's all well and good, but it cost me $35,000 in legal and accounting fees to fight the case. The IRS abuse was overwhelming, and I understood that agents get paid bonuses on amounts collected. I won the case, but I still got beat. I worked hard to build a company and keep six people employed, and the IRS ends up destroying your enthusiasm. Never to be beaten down, I forged ahead.

Chapter Seven

THE SERIAL ENTREPRENEUR

PALM BEACH POLO

I met an attorney in Denver who played Polo and wanted insurance for his Polo ponies. At the time, I didn't have a program to provide coverage for horses that were used for Polo, but with Lloyds of London, anything was possible. After a few telexes' back and forth, I had contract from Lloyds to insure his ponies.

The attorney told me of his love for the sport, and his ponies. I always had this desire to play Polo, and my new client told me about a Polo school in Denver, that was all I needed. I started taking lessons at the Denver Polo Club headed up by an Iranian fellow by the name of John Gandomcar. John was responsible for introducing hundreds of players to the sport. I managed to get several lessons under my belt, and like so many players, I got hooked! I purchased my first horse from John. Many people would ask me why I got into Polo, and my response to jokingly justify the growing addiction, I would laugh and say.

"It was a divorce present to myself!"

Later that winter, I traveled to Palm Beach, Florida to attend a Polo school at the Palm Beach Polo and Country Club (PBPCC). The school instructor was Major Hugh Dawnay. He formerly was the captain of the British military team reaching the rank of Major in the British Army 10th Royal Hussars. After leaving the Army, Major Dawnay formed coaching clinics and schools in fifteen different countries, including ten Polo clinics every year during the winter season at PBPCC.

The first time I arrived at PBPCC, I thought that I had died and gone to heaven. There were eleven Polo fields on the property, and everything got groomed to perfection. The Polo clubhouse, called the *Players Club*, was like something out of a James Bond movie; dark mahogany wood, English racing green carpet, a beautiful bar and restaurant with brass fixtures, and photos that lined the walls with all the top players and celebrity players from around the world.

The clinic started on Monday and finished on Sunday. The class was rewarded with free tickets to watch the high goal game played on the number one field. This is where I would first shake the hand of the future President, Donald J. Trump.

Donald Trump with his first wife Ivana. Presenting the winning trophy to Henryk de Kwaitkowski and rest of the Kennelot Polo Team.

Mr. Trump and his first wife, Ivanna, would frequently attend the Sunday matches at PBPCC, and Trump often threw out the first ball. PBPCC was famous for drawing celebrities from all over the country to take in the festivities and start the game with a throw-in from the back of a shiny new Cadillac

Allante. Donald and Ivana Trump, Princess Diana, and Prince Charles are just two examples of high society mavens called on to start the matches and throw in the first ball.

There were also numerous celebrities who played Polo. They would gather annually to play in charity Polo matches at Palm Beach Polo. Sylvester Stallone, Bill Devane, Stephanie Powers, Tommy Lee Jones, and Doug Sheehan, would take to the field and thrill the crowd. I remember getting asked to lend Stephanie Powers two of my horses for a celebrity match. We went out for a ride together the day before her match, so that she could try out my horses. It was a great experience to spend time with this beautiful and gracious lady.

Reflecting back, I recall the first day of the Polo clinic; we gathered at the Players Club at 8 am., Major Dawnay started with some chalkboard instruction. One of the students, a lawyer from New York City, had not shown up but we started anyway.

Now you must understand, Major Dawnay ran the school like a military boot camp. Starting on time was imperative, and being late was not something you wanted to do. The New York lawyer showed up at 8:15 a.m. and the Major scolded him like a plebian private and rode him hard all day long. Knowing that I was German, he called me the "Hard Headed Kraut".

The best Polo instructor in the world
Major Hugh Dawnay

Like a drill sergeant, he would scream at me, "You hard headed Kruat, I can't teach you anything. I can't tell if you are dumb or just hard headed!" Like a good private, I kept my mouth shut and stared at the Major with my usual German-like glare manifesting no visible emotion.

On the second day of the clinic, the lawyer showed up at 8:30 a.m. Wow! The major got pissed. He yelled at the lawyer all day long. On the third day, the lawyer quit, and never showed his face again. The Major just laughed. "What do I care, the moron had paid all of his money up front, so it's his loss," he told us boastfully.

We learned to ride in military formation, it may seem strange, but it teaches you a fundamental element of the Polo game. After the third day, Major Dawnay asked us if we wanted to play some chukkers (a period in a Polo match) at a private field, I immediately agreed. I didn't know whose field it was, but it was a beautiful farm, close to Palm Beach Polo. Two experienced players played the match with us, they weren't part of the school, and we had one on each side. The Major explained that they would captain each team to help keep the ball moving. The horses (ponies they're called) were well-trained. When someone hit a back shot, the pony automatically turned on a dime in the opposite direction before I could even think about turning for the back shot. They were so quick about it, I remember clearly almost going over the front end of my pony on several occasions.

The better player assigned to my team was amazing, he would hit the ball and it would land perfectly in front of me. I was astonished by the accuracy. But, when we finished playing, I finally figured out who we were playing Polo with. My team had Gonzalo Pieres, he came with a 10-goal handicap and was one of the best players in the world. I felt a little stupid because a 10-goal handicap is considered a perfect player. It is also the top handicap that a player can achieve. When I started playing Polo, there were only ten, 10-goal players in the world. My excitement was difficult to contain after learning that playing on the other team was Gonzalo's 9-goal cousin. That is like playing golf with Tiger Woods and Arnold Palmer at the height of their careers!

To end the clinic, we attended the Sunday match with the Major. There was a lot of buzz going on as to why the game got delayed. We heard that they were waiting for Deborah Couples to arrive. She was the patron of one of the high goal teams playing that Sunday, and the wife of the notable PGA champion, Fred Couples. She showed up about fifteen minutes late but never made it to her horse. A Palm Beach Sheriff car followed her into the club, and they hauled her off in handcuffs. I later learned that she got stopped for speeding on her way to the club. The story spread quickly . . . when she got pulled over, the narcissistic Couples acted far from polite to the officer.

"Officer, I don't have time to answer your stupid questions," she yelled. "Don't you know who I am?" Couples asked.

"No madam, you could be the First Lady, but I don't give a damn," the officer told her while waiting for her identification.

"Well, many people do, and I happen to be on my way to a very important Polo match," she continued to berate him while rummaging through her handbag. "Here is my license and insurance . . . you need to hurry up!" she yelled at him.

The officer went back to his car shaking his head. He was about to check her license, when he heard Couples start her engine and speed off, racing to the Polo club. Not a good plan. The officer followed her, lights flashing and siren blazing, right into the club where she was then apprehended and taken to jail. They found a substitute for Deborah and the game played on. The Palm Sheriff's Department has never been persuadable by anyone's celebrity or monetary status. This was a memorable experience with a lot of excitement for my last day of the clinic.

After returning home I got thinking about my Polo experience, Major Dawnay's school had impressed me. I made plans to return three more times to enjoy the amazing fields and incredible horses, not to mention the Major's astonishing ability to coach and improve my game.

Each time I went back to Palm Beach I would buy a horse. Many of my horses at that time were bred and imported from Argentina. I purchased three horses from Henryk de Kwiatkowski. An interesting man who owned the Kennelot Polo Team and the famed Calumet Thoroughbred horse racing and breeding farm in Lexington, Kentucky. Kwiatkowski hired several Argentine pros to play his horses and lead his team to major tournament wins. Henryk would buy horses for $60,000 to $100,000 for his high-goal team.

He hired the best pros, Eduardo, and Bautista Heguy to play in tournaments with him. Bautista rated 10-goals and Eduardo 9-goals at that time. They would play the ponies hard for two or three years, then they got sold to lower goal players like me who would play them for at least a few more years in lower goal tournaments.

The horses lasted me for five more years versus, if they would continue the rigors of high goal tournaments, they might only last another year. Amazing horses that Henryk had purchased for $60,000, I would then pick them up for $10,000 or $15,000. I can never forget Madonna, she turned out to be the best horse I ever owned, and she came from Kennelot and was played in many high-goal tournaments by Bautista Heguy.

The best Polo Mare I ever owned
"Madonna"
purchsed from
Henryk de Kwiatkowski

Chapter Eight

THE SERIAL ENTREPRENEUR

FIELD OF DREAMS

My Polo was getting serious; I had grown to a full string of Polo ponies boarded at the Denver Polo Club, which got to be very expensive. My insurance company was doing well, and it became time to purchase my own farm. I found a five-acre piece of vacant land south of downtown Denver in Greenwood Village, Colorado, and even though it was in the middle of a major population area, the land came with zoning rights for horses. I paid $150,000 for the vacant land.

I had been so impressed with Kwiatkowski's barn in Palm Beach, FL, I wanted a barn just like that one. I flew to Palm Beach and took detailed photos of Henryk's barn. Every nook and cranny was photographed so I could replicate his masterpiece. After returning, I met with the architect and instructed him not to deviate from the photographs. Construction started in the spring of 1990. I did most of the work myself along with the help of my friend Steve Rogoff. Steve was a master builder and taught me much about construction.

The city wanted to charge me $60,000 to bring water to the property. On top of that huge upfront cost, I didn't want to have a big water bill every month, because along with the barn, I naturally wanted my own Polo practice field, and that requires an enormous amount of water each month. I hired a drilling company to drill a private well for $15,000. After 800 feet, we hit a gusher. We ran into a problem; the city would only allow me to put a 4-hp motor on the pump. That would have been fine if I was only going supply water for the horses and the living quarters that I was building for myself, but I needed to water an entire Polo field! A Polo field (300 by 160 yards) is equivalent to three football fields. Although my practice Polo field would be smaller, with that little motor it would take three days to water my field, not to mention there would never be enough pressure to water it properly.

I came up with a great solution. I found a company that refurbishes large gasoline tanks that were removed from closed gas stations. The tanks were relined and cleaned. I knew the city would never allow such a tank to be buried on the property, especially when the mayor of Greenwood Village lived in a house located at the entrance of the road leading to my property. Here is my devious solution to the problem: First we dug a big hole for the tank, and the next night a large flat-bed semi-trailer truck quietly slipped past the Mayor's house and delivered the tank. By the next morning, the 15,000-gallon tank had disappeared. It got buried in the ground and out of sight. I put a large 40-hp motor on the tank to water the Polo field. Now we could slowly fill the tank with the 4-hp motor from the well and use the tank water to irrigate the entire field in less than three hours.

My property turned into a "Field of Dreams" in the middle of the city. Once the Polo field got completed, Steve Rogoff and I began construction on the barn and living quarters. The ceiling in the living quarters was thirty feet high. Putting up 8-foot drywall panels thirty feet in the air was a real bitch, so when we finished, we agreed that it was a good idea to hire someone to mud and sand the drywall.

The Barn & Polo Field that KT&T built.

There is a facility, *Step 13* in Denver, for alcohol and drug rehab. It has high regard as a great program. They allow the attendees to work during the day and ask that you pay them $5 per hour in cash. You must pick them up at 9 a.m. and have them back by 6 p.m. I found a guy who used to be a drywall professional in New York City, we lucked out!

One afternoon I left the office and went to the farm. I wanted to check on the progress of the man I had left to work on the stable's living quarters. When I opened the door and walked in, I found myself surrounded by an abundance of drywall dust from the guy sanding the drywall. I couldn't even see my own hand in front of my face.

"Hey, Mike! Are you in here somewhere?" I called out.

"Yeah over here," he replied.

I followed the sound of his voice and finally found him through the dust; he looked like a ghost covered from head to toe in dust. His foot-long beard was covered with the white material, and low and behold sticking out of his mouth, was a non-filtered Camel cigarette.

"Mike, why in the hell don't you have a mask on?" I asked, feeling concerned for this man's lungs.

"Nah, don't need one, I'm used to this."

"Aren't you worried about getting cancer or lung disease from all the dust and those Camel cigarettes you're smoking?"

"This isn't nearly as bad as when I did drywall in New York City. Those drywall panels had asbestos in them," he proclaimed.

"Whatever you say," I quipped. "Okay, Mike I need to get out of here before I choke to death."

"See you, boss!"

Driving away I felt genuinely concerned. I was getting cheap labor, but was I adding to the demise of this talented man who was trying to get his life back on track? The experience gave me pause to be grateful for my life.

Chapter Nine

THE SERIAL ENTREPRENEUR

NOT ALL MODELS ARE PRETTY

Donna Baldwin Talent is the premier talent agency in Denver. They represent actors and models for commercials, ads, fashion shows, voiceovers, live events, and promotions. One morning arriving at my office, I was told that Donna Baldwin wanted to speak with me. Naturally, I knew of her agency, but was surprised. *What could she possibly want from me,* I thought as I picked up the telephone.

She was very gracious as we exchanged pleasantries, then she asked if the agency could do a photo shoot using my Polo field, my horses as well as me, and some other players as a backdrop. Of course, I immediately agreed. *Why not hang out with beautiful women for an afternoon.* I thought.

The photo shoot took some organizing on my part, but I felt it was good advertising for my "Field of Dreams". When we finished, Donna asked me an unexpected question.

"Robert, have ever done any modeling?"

"N-no," I said, a little taken aback.

"Would like to?" she asked. Of course, I felt flattered, and at thirty-five I thought that I may be little old, but she insisted that I could get a lot of work.

"Robert, I feel that your total look is rather unique, and I'm always on the lookout for a different theme."

"Well, if you think so my answer is yes, where do I sign?" I smiled.

My first job was for a skincare line commercial. What great fun this was! As Bob Dole once said, *"It's an indoor Job without too much heavy lifting and toting."* Modeling was a great diversion from my normal life. You got to be someone else for a day, and the pay wasn't too bad either. I received $1,200 for the skincare commercial and that was a single days work.

I ended up doing a lot of print jobs for Donna Baldwin. I became the face of Lawrence Covell, a high-end men's and women's store in Denver. Needless to say, modeling was great fun, and I could have worked five days per week, but I had three other businesses to run.

Nevertheless, I took jobs two or three days each week. The usual pay was $125 to $300 per hour, not too shabby for my ugly mug.

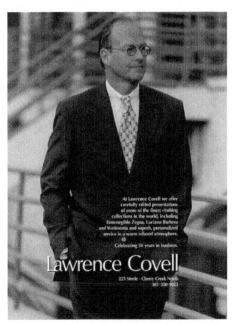

I met a beautiful model, also employed by Baldwin Talent. After dating her for a while, I learned she had been one of the girls involved in the extramarital carnal knowledge with Bill Cosby.

I must say that I was confused. She admitted to me that she previously had a consensual sexual relationship with Cosby when he would come to town.

Robert Kiger on the set of the
Skincare Commercial

Ultimately years later, she became one of the many women joining Gloria Allred's list of accusers against Cosby, claiming he had drugged her after she had visited him in his Denver dressing room. Difficult to believe after admitting to having consensual sex. She told me that she had woke up in her car, not remembering how she got there. All of her clothes were messed up and her bra was unhooked. It wasn't until 2006, a decade later, that she came forward to tell her story. Who am I to Judge?

I continued modeling when I went to Palm Beach securing a contract with an agency in Miami Beach. It was great fun to be pampered for a few hours a week. But, it got to be too much driving to Miami three and sometimes four times per week. In addition, the modeling agency owed me thousands of dollars and they weren't paying due to financial problems. I was spending too much time away from my business, so I stopped modeling, and my pampering days came to an end.

Chapter Ten

THE SERIAL ENTREPRENEUR

GIVING BACK

Kiger & Associates was doing well. I had worked hard, and it was time to reward myself. I decided to buy a new Jaguar. I met Kent Stevenson the owner of Stevenson Automotive; he had eight dealerships in and around Denver. I received a call from Kent that my car had arrived, I hurried down anxious to first get a glimpse, and secondly, get behind the wheel of this shiny new black, Jaguar XJ6.

After taking my Jaguar around the town for a test run, I came back to the dealership to clear up the paperwork. Kent and I began chatting; he shared with me his idea of creating a charity to benefit disadvantaged children in Colorado. He wanted me to join him in this endeavor. After much discussion, Kent asked me if I thought it was a good idea, and if I would be willing to be a founding member. My answer was, "Absolutely". We decided to call it The *Denver Active 20/30*. It would become a chartered-chapter of the long-standing *Active 20/30 International* organization established in 1922. The members were men in their twenties and thirties (hence the name) who would ultimately become leaders in the community.

The state charter finally got approved, and the *Denver Active 20/30* was now ready to raise money. We received great interest and invited another handful of guys to join us for the first meeting. The first goal in front of us was trying to decide what kind of fundraisers we could hold. I suggested that we could have a charity Polo match. Most thought it was a good idea, but the match would be June 30th, and it was already May 15th. No one thought that we could pull it off in forty-five days. I heard their concerns and gave my justification for giving it a shot.

"We are having the Polo match anyway, so if we don't make any money, we have nothing to lose," I told them. They agreed to the concept, and we were on our way to organizing our first charity Polo match. We didn't want to risk spending money on a caterer, so we enlisted the wives and girlfriends to bring a dish, and help with the food. They were real troopers, spending hours chopping vegetables, and preparing great finger food.

I remember watching the display of food set out for the event and smiled to myself giving credence to a long-standing idiom, "Behind every good man is a great woman." The work we did on advertising and getting the word out paid off, we attracted a big crowd, the weather couldn't have been more perfect, and everyone had a great time. The first annual *Denver Polo Classic* was exciting and at the end of the day, we raised $600. Not bad for the naysayers to see the myth come to fruition once again, "Build it and they will come!"

Kent's dream got bigger and better every year. The *Denver Active 20/30* is still going strong. Now in its 30th year (2018), the non-profit organization is comprised of over one hundred young men who volunteer a substantial amount of time to raise money on behalf of disadvantaged, at-risk youth in our local community. The *DA20/30* is known for hosting world-class events that combine five-star service and top-tier fun for guests.

It was a proud day for both Kent and me when in 1993 I participated in the *Denver Polo Classic* tournament and my

Kent Stevinson Presenting the Best Playing Pony Award to Robert Kiger at the 6th Annual Denver Polo Classic

team won the match! I received the Best Playing Pony award and was handed the Stevinson Lexus/Jaguar Award from Kent himself.

The *Denver Polo Classic* is now the nation's largest charitable Polo tournament. Held over the course of three days at the legendary Polo Reserve in Littleton, CO – the *Denver Polo Classic* is *Denver Active 20/30's* premiere event, offering a unique experience complete with world-class Polo players and thousands of guests from across the metro area.

The first Polo match raised a few hundred dollars. Now, looking back, it's gratifying for Kent and I, along with the rest of the founding members to know how far the organization has come. The *Denver Polo Classic* combined with matching funds from the Nuggets Foundation, the McCormick Foundation, and other organizations, raise more than one million dollars during the three-day event.

Chapter Eleven

THE SERIAL ENTREPRENEUR

BACK TO PALM BEACH

In the fall of 1991, I decided to take the horses to Palm Beach for the season to play tournament Polo. I convinced my good friend Scott Southworth to make the trip with me. He agreed and on October 15th, we left the freezing cold Denver weather, loaded up the truck, the ten horse trailer, and headed south. We made our first stop in Wichita Falls, Texas. We pulled into a vacant lot in a truck stop to let the horses out for feed and water.

It has gone down to ten degrees below zero and the wind was blowing thirty m.p.h. and we were freezing our butts off. I joked to Scott, *"Buddy, it is so cold out here, you have to jam a stick up your ass and holler SNAKE! Just to see your nuts"*

Scott laughed, "I'm not sure that would even work in this weather!"

The wind was blowing so hard that when we put the hay on the ground it immediately blew away. We had to feed the horses hay while holding it in our hands. We finally loaded up and continued the journey east.

Our next stop was Shreveport Louisiana. It was pouring down rain, but I saw a sign for the State Fairgrounds and figured there must be a spot where we could let the horses out for exercise and feeding. I tried the door to the indoor arena and was shocked that it was unlocked at 9 p.m. Thank God we had found some cover. We quickly let the horses out and saw to it they had water, grain, and hay, then jumped back in the truck to stay dry while they did their thing. Forty minutes went by, the rain had started to ease up a little, and we decided to get the hell out of there before anyone saw us. But we were wrong!

While we were loading the horses back into the trailer, we were met by the State Police with rain gear on and flashlights in their hand. "What the hell do you think you are doing?" The officer asked, shining the flashlight in my face.

"Sorry officer, we have been on the road for twenty-eight hours, and the horses needed food and shelter," I explained.

"You can be charged with trespassing, and breaking and entering," he threatened.

"W-when I tried the door it was unlocked, and I immediately took advantage of the situation for the poor horses, we didn't mean to cause any harm," I pleaded, with a little drama added to my voice. Scott continued to load the last two horses, and as he closed the trailer door I looked at the officers waiting for the verdict.

"Okay, get the hell out of here, and next time plan your trip a little better. This arena is not meant for public use," he said. They turned off the flashlights and headed for their patrol car. Scott and I quickly got into the truck and were on our way before they even pulled away. We were relieved that this was the last leg of our trip.

The drive from Denver to Palm Beach, in a car, is normally thirty-six hours non-stop. But, with a truck, towing a 36ft. trailer with a full load of horses, it takes more than forty hours. When we reached the Florida state line I had been driving for thirty hours. I told Scott, "I can't stay awake any longer, you have to drive." He had never driven a truck and trailer before. I pulled the old Terry Cotton trick, and told him, "Just keep it between the lines and drive fifty-five miles an hour, it's a straight shot."

I felt like I had only just got to sleep when Scott started to shake me, yelling,

"Wake up, Wake up!"

When I came to my senses, I saw police lights flashing and sirens blazing.

"What the hell did you do, Scott?" I asked. The cops came to the window and informed us we had blown through an Agricultural Weigh Station forty-five miles back.

Scott and I were both shiting our pants. I knew about the Agricultural Station, but being so tired I completely forgot to tell Scott.

"I could make you boys turn around and back-track the forty-five miles to the Weigh Station," the officer harshly declared. But lucky for us, he must have been in a sympathetic mood that night. He proceeded to inspect our Health Papers and Coggins Certificates comparing descriptions with the horses on the side of the interstate.

The Agricultural Station is specifically situated near the border to make sure that horses entering Florida had not been stolen, and each horse had their own health inspection certificate to ensure no diseases were coming into the state. We finally arrived at Palm Beach Polo at 10 a.m., got the horses fed and bedded down. Then it was time for us to get an over-due shower and rest.

The season was everything I could hope for. My horses went well and I had the chance to play Polo with many high-goal players. It improved my game tremendously. I fell in love with Palm Beach Polo so much, when I went back to Denver after the season, I decided to move Kiger & Associates to Palm Beach. I asked Suzy Stasko, a good friend of mine in the real estate business to find a buyer for my Denver property. I told her that I wanted to list the property for $775,000, and she could put it on the MLS, but no road signs.

"Kiger you're nuts, at that price, it will never sell," Suzy told me. Three days later I had a cash offer for $750,000. I had invested $350,000 in the property including the improvements. I sold my "Field of Dreams" and used the money to purchase a condo in The Palm Beach Polo and Country Club.

After settling the sale of my property, I moved my insurance office into a space located above the Palm Beach Polo stadium. The situation was perfect, my condo that backed up to the number one field at PBPCC was a two-minute golf cart ride to the office. I could leave the office, jump on my golf cart, play a Polo match and head back to the office in quick order to make more money so I could play more Polo. They say Polo is like an addictive drug. The only thing that will make you stop playing Polo is poverty or death.

When I wasn't working or playing Polo, I was transfixed to the media frenzy that was gripping the entire nation. Nicole Brown and Ronald Goldman were brutally murdered on the

O.J. Simpson estate on June 12, 1994, and the case fascinated me. The trial began January 24, 1995, I taped the entire day's court proceedings and would go home and watch sometimes until three in the morning. This went on every day until October 3, 1995. My friend Jason Blood worked for me at Kiger and Associates, and we were anxiously waiting for the verdict to come in.

On that day, we had scheduled a meeting in North Florida. Driving along we were listening to the court proceedings on the radio. Just as they were announcing the verdict, we pulled under a toll booth on the Florida Turnpike and lost the radio signal. We didn't get to hear the verdict! After paying the turnpike fees, we got rolling again, the radio signal came back, and the announcer kept saying, "I can't believe this, I can't believe this", and wouldn't repeat what the verdict was. We had been watching for ten months, and now missed the final result. We finally heard the verdict, and I wasn't surprised.

The trial of the century was over. The dream team was victorious; O.J. got acquitted on both counts of murder. Now, I know we all think O.J. was guilty, but if I were sitting on the jury, I would have never voted to convict. It was a colossal failure of the prosecution to present a case devoid of Reasonable Doubt. I also believed that Barry Scheck, the defense DNA expert, obliterated LA Police Department Lab findings. In my opinion, this was the determining factor in the acquittal of O.J.

Chapter Twelve

THE SERIAL ENTREPRENEUR

THE SCHECK SHOCK

After doing some consulting work for a telecommunications company called, *IdealDial*, in Denver, Colorado I got offered a permanent position as Vice President of Telecom Services. I decided to sell my insurance business in June of 1996 and move back to Denver.

I took a loft downtown on 17th Street, which was around the corner from the Federal Courthouse. On April 24th, 1997, opening statements were being presented in the Timothy McVeigh trial for the 1995 Murrah Federal Building bombing in Oklahoma City. The tragedy had claimed the lives of 168 innocent victims, injuring more than 600 others.

A change of venue got ordered to Denver fearing that McVeigh would not receive a fair trial in Oklahoma. I was now living half a block from the U.S. District Court House where the trial would be held. The entire prosecution team, the defense team, and an army of media folks were staying in a hotel across the street from me. Federal agents in blacked-out SUV's were stationed on every side of my loft and the hotel. I never felt safer in my life as I did when the trial was going on.

One morning while walking to my office, I spotted Barry Scheck from the O.J. court case. He was one of the commentators for the McVeigh trial. I walked up to Scheck extending my hand and asked if I could meet him. He shook my hand, and I introduced myself.

"Mr. Scheck, I intently watched you during the O.J. trial," I began, but immediately I could see the manifestation of a shitty look coming across his face. I could tell what he was thinking. *Oh, shit! Here we go again!* That wasn't my idea to start criticizing him for defending O.J.

"Mr. Scheck, I was in awe and amazed by your brilliance in the courtroom," I said, "I have never seen anything like it. You single-handedly saved Simpson.

Because of your defense, if I had been sitting on the jury, I would have voted for acquittal."

"Wow! That is not usually what I get. I was expecting another verbal attack!" Barry smiled.

The Oklahoma City bombing was the worst domestic terror attack in U.S history. Unfortunately, that would soon change.

Chapter Thirteen

THE SERIAL ENTREPRENEUR

KIGER TELEPHONE

Working as vice-president for *IdealDial*, I got to know more about Doug Hanson, the primary shareholder of Rocky Mountain Internet. I learned that he was also the creator of SP Telecommunications. Doug had a brilliant idea of burying fiber optic cable along railroad rights-of-way throughout the United States. He later sold SP Telecom to Philip Anschutz, which then became Qwest Communications.

Hanson served as the first President and CEO of Qwest. Doug was instrumental in creating the first public offering, achieving a market cap in excess of $1 billion. Phillip Anschutz, the Chairman of the Board of Qwest, decided he needed a Wall Street guy to lead the company to the next level.

The new CEO, Joe Nacchio, was the *Big Wall Street Guy*, who replaced Hanson. A decision that would later prove to be a very poor strategic move. In 2007, Nacchio got convicted on nineteen counts of insider trading of Qwest stock in 2007.

When Hanson left Qwest, he walked away with $12 million severance compensation. He used a portion of that money to obtain controlling interest in Rocky Mountain Internet (RMI). When Doug purchased RMI, it was a small local internet company (ISP) with $4 million in annual revenue. Through his leadership, Hanson grew the company in four short years to revenue in excess of $70 million annually.

Doug was gobbling up a vast number of small ISP's across the country, and in 1998 *IdealDial* got sold to Hanson's Rocky Mountain Internet. Except for some of the customer service staff, all *IdealDial* employees, including me, were fired. I asked for a meeting with Hanson to plead my case to keep my job. I asked him to allow me to work for thirty days for free, if at the end of that period, I had proved to be valuable to the company, he could give me a permanent position. He agreed, and when thirty days had passed, I was offered a Director position for $36,000 per year. That was a substantial decrease from my $120,000 per year salary I had with *IdealDial.* Shortly thereafter, the woman that headed up the telecom division for RMI left the company, and I got promoted to Vice President of Telecommunications Services for Rocky Mountain Internet.

I figured that I had finally made it. I was on the top floor of the 17th Street Plaza that was home to only RMI VP's. None the less, titles are cheap. My annual salary did rise to $60,000 per year: however, it was still 50% of what my annual salary was twelve months prior. I grew the division to one of the only profitable divisions in the company and continued to renegotiate my contract. I had excellent negotiating leverage, since other than Hanson, I was the only one in the company who knew anything about telecommunications. Within twelve months I had negotiated my salary and commissions back to $120,000. I also received stock options, and if the stock price had remained at $12 per share, my package would be worth $4 million when the options matured in five years.

RMI became Internet Commerce & Communications. Doug had continued to buy more regional ISP's. In my opinion, the rapid growth would eventually bring about the demise of IC&C.

After spending $1.5 million dollars with Oracle, they were never able to successfully integrate the billing system across more than fifty regional ISP's that Doug had purchased. Billing was a mess, and customer service was flooded with calls. Hanson insisted I switch the Telecom Billing System over to the Oracle platform.

"Over my dead body! I will resign if you make me do that." Because of the complexity of the telecom billing system, I knew that switching to the new billing platform would be a disaster. Doug never made me switch.

Although, IC&C was grossing $70 million per year they were burning through $1.5 million net loss per month. There were 650 employees of IC&C. In the spring of 1998, in a desperate effort to lower costs, the other VP's and I were to cut staff by two hundred people. Soon that proved to not be enough, so another hundred had to be cut. The company continued to bleed cash. The staff cuts continued, ISP services and particularly customer service was now a thing of the past. Six months later it was announced that IC&C would file for bankruptcy. Suddenly, my $4 million in stock options were not worth the paper they were printed on.

One of the hardest things I have ever done was to fire a countless number of people from the company. I had to sit across the desk and watch grown men and women cry as their future got decimated. It was so sad to tell a woman who was eight months pregnant she would no longer have health insurance. When the company finally closed its doors, I was one of six people that were still on the payroll.

With defeat came an opportunity for me. Doug Hanson, the man I admired for so long, who I considered a great mentor, did me a huge favor. He made arrangements for me to purchase the telecom division out of bankruptcy. Thus, Kiger Telephone & Telephony was born. I named it KT&T because it sounded so much like AT&T when the receptionist answered the phone. I purchased the entire customer base, the billing system, and all of the hardware for basically the cost of the switching equipment. Pennies on the dollar!

Kiger Telephone and Telephony took space on the 18th floor of the 17th Street Plaza. The first goal was to build out the data center. In 1999 the computers and switching equipment were much larger than the equipment today. The racks of machines generated enormous heat, so the air conditioning in the room had to be extensive. I got the $40,000 AC unit installed, and we were up and running. Along with the usual long distance services, and pre-paid calling cards, KT&T had a lot of IVR (interactive voice response) clients. We were one of those annoying companies that created telephony programs that made you talk to a computer when you called a 1-800 number in lieu of talking to a live customer service representative.

Then came September 11th, 2001, I woke at 6:30 a.m. MST to start my day, flicked on Fox News, and like all Americans, I was horrified by the images on the TV screen. American flight 11 had just crashed into the North Tower of the World Trade Center at 8:46 a.m. EDT. Glued to the TV set, seventeen minutes later, I watched as United Airlines Flight 175 hit the South Tower. At 9:31 a.m., President Bush addressed the nation from an Elementary school in Sarasota

Florida, calling the events an "Apparent terrorist attack on our country."

The reports were coming in that other major cities in the U.S., Los Angeles, Chicago, and Denver may be in danger of an attack. Worried about my own staff's safety, I headed to the office. The 17th Street Plaza was a significant telecom hub housing numerous data centers, as well as offices for the FBI. When I arrived security personnel and FBI agents were in the lobby. They were locking down the building and did not want to allow me to go to my office. I explained that I just wanted to go up and send my staff home. They agreed and I sent everyone home. I stayed in my office and continued to watch the agonizing events unfold as hijackers aboard Flight 77 crashed into the Pentagon, then the collapse of the South Tower, at 10:07 a.m., the deliberate crash of Flight 93 in Somerset County Pennsylvania, the collapse of the North Tower at 10:28 a.m., and finally, 5:20 p.m. the fall of Seven World Trade Center. The nightmare of the day's terrorist activities was now over and the hard work began. Finding those dirty bastards responsible for these unthinkable acts of terror was paramount.

Ten days later, my administrative assistant came running into my office in a panic. "We are getting sued by the FBI, and the United States Secret Service," she screamed. "It's right here in black and white, look at these faxes!" She handed them to me.

"Sit down and catch your breath," I told her while I looked quickly at what she handed me. "This is a subpoena asking us to supply them call records for specific phone numbers," I grinned. The first list had approximately thirty numbers on it. I knew that we could run these numbers through our database to see if any of them hit our switching equipment.

Sure enough, we found three numbers that were on their subpoena. They were from prepaid calling cards that we had sold to American Express. The prepaid cards had ten minutes free long-distance calling on them. American Express would distribute the free cards as gifts for promotional purposes.

We could supply the FBI the date and time of the call, the origination point, the termination point, as well as the duration of the call. We found that all the calls originated from Florida.

Over the course of the next two months, we would receive several more subpoenas. *What an amazing Secret Service and FBI we have,* I thought, *they leave no stone unturned.* The detail of the FBI investigation was impressive. Searching out a tiny telecom company like KT&T, and tracking down each phone call of suspected terrorists was outstanding. I felt proud that my company could support their efforts.

Chapter Fourteen

THE SERIAL ENTREPRENEUR

FASHION & KT&T POLO

I developed a great interest in fashion due to my experience in modeling and in the back of my head I had always thought about owning a clothing boutique. Cherry Creek was five miles from downtown Denver. All the high-end shops were in this area. It was the Worth Avenue or Rodeo Drive of Denver. So, in 2002 I decided it was time to make that happen and I searched for a space in Cherry Creek.

I found a 2,000 sq. ft. space next to a high-traffic Starbucks. I signed the contract and began the fun part, the buildout. Other store owners would come by and say, "Who is the designer?" They were shocked when I told them that I was the designer. Doing the work myself was exceptionally gratifying.

Working day and night, the construction was completed in sixty days. It was a prodigious opening-day for my Polo Gear store, and I was finally able to cut the ribbon with the executives from the Merchants Association.

When customers walked in it was as if they had arrived at a Ralph Lauren store, complete with free-flowing champagne. A 10-foot movie screen consumed the entire back wall of the store where we played non-stop Polo films and fashion shows.

My time got split between the Polo Gear store and KT&T, but I was still anxious to take on more responsibility, so I purchased half interest in the Willow Creek Polo Club southeast of Denver. The 60-acre parcel was large enough for two Polo fields and a stick and ball practice field. I also purchased a 17-acre parcel contiguous to the Polo fields. I was able to accommodate my eight Polo ponies along with lush turnout fields to board another thirty ponies for visiting teams.

The KT&T Polo Facility and Willow Creek Polo Club

I ran the Willow Creek Polo Club on the property and we had about fifty members, but the most notable was Rick Lontin and David Starman. They were two big, tough guys on and off the Polo field. I will never forget the incident that happened with those guys. After we had played a Polo match, David and Rick decided to head to a local bar for some refreshments. They were still wearing their Polo jerseys and white Polo pants. Inside the bar was a group of Hells Angel-like bikers drinking at a large table. When Rick and Dave walked by their table, the bikers started to laugh and point at them, then one biker called Rick a faggot. Well, all hell broke loose as that comment wasn't received kindly by either of them. Within seconds, Rick picked up a chair and cracked it over the bikers head. The brawl ensued. They were outnumbered six to two and it wasn't a pretty sight. They got beat up pretty bad, the police arrived and everyone went to jail.

The brawl occurred on a Saturday afternoon, so it was a long weekend for Rick and Dave, as they didn't have to appear in court until Monday morning. My friend Todd McIntosh happened to be the Deputy District Attorney for the 18th Judicial District in Arapahoe County. He was a member of the *Denver Active 20/30* and I knew him well. He would be hearing the case, and decide if they would be held over for trial.

On Monday morning, McIntosh asked Rick to tell his version of Saturday's event. Rick explained that they had just come from a Polo match, minding their own business, when the bikers called them faggots. Rick said he couldn't let that one go unanswered.

"You were coming from a Polo match?" Deputy DA

Macintosh asked.

"Yes, your honor," Rick responded.

"You play Polo?" He asked.

"Yes, your honor." Rick began to wonder what he was getting at.

"Do you know Robert Kiger?" Macintosh asked. Rick took his time before answering, deciding whether to take the risk.

"Before I answer your honor. Will that help or hurt me?" Rick grinned nervously.

Barely able to compose his laughter, McIntosh told them they were free to go with time well served.

Chapter Fifteen

THE SERIAL ENTREPRENEUR

THE LOOPHOLE THAT SAVED ME

Although I was doing quite well, a beautiful girlfriend, a Polo club, a telecom company, and an awesome clothing store, something seemed to be missing. It kept gnawing at me, and then the epiphany hit me, I had no faith in my life.

I decided that I wanted to join the Catholic Church. I had three marriages and three divorces under my belt, so I thought to join the church was virtually impossible. It didn't prohibit me from attending Mass, but I could never take communion. The Holy Ghost Church was a block away from my office in downtown Denver. It was an amazing Cathedral. Although the present Holy Ghost Church was dedicated on July 8, 1943, the parish has its roots in the 1860 construction of St. Mary's Cathedral, the first Catholic Church in Denver. I liked the tradition, discipline, and formality of the church. I began attending Mass every morning at 7:30 a.m., and I could be in my office by 8:15 a.m., it was a good way to start my day.

After about two weeks of attending daily Mass, the priest came to me and introduced himself. "I see you attending Mass every day, why do you not take communion?" he asked. Full of embarrassment, I told him of my puerilely and failure of three marriages. "Why don't you come and see me. We can talk about it?" he offered

We arranged to meet the next day. During the meeting, we prayed together, and then he started asking me questions about my religious past. He asked me if my parents were churchgoing folks.

"No, but they had found God late in life, and were members of the Lutheran Church several years before they died," I told him.

"Did you join the Lutheran Church, or have you ever attended churches of different denominations?"

"Only for my marriages and weddings of others," I admitted.

"Were you ever married in a Catholic Church or have

you ever been baptized in a church?" he asked.

"No, I have not."

A smile came across his face. "Son, you haven't been born yet! Since you have never been baptized, all your indiscretions, marriages and divorces in the past are not recognized by God or the church," he told me.

The priest and the Catholic Church had just given me a rebirth and a second chance at life. We set up private catechism classes for me two times per week. Four months later, I got baptized at the Holy Ghost church, and received my first communion. My long-time pal, Kent Stevenson, a life-long Catholic, agreed to be my Godfather. It was a joyous day, and at the same time, it was strange to be a 45-year-old man sharing a baptism ceremony with three babies.

Prior to Christmas, the church would hold a special Mass for poverty-stricken citizens of Denver. They would hand out $50 to every man, women, and child during the crowded mass. A family of four could receive $200 to spend on gifts or Christmas dinner. I was honored to be one of the parishioners selected to distribute the money to these deserving folks. I will never forget the look in the eyes of a seven-year-old boy when I handed him a crisp, new $50 bill, and he told me, "Thank you, I can finally buy my mother and father a Christmas present."

I will always be thankful for joining the church. Christmastime was an extraordinary experience at the Holy Ghost Church.

Chapter Sixteen

THE SERIAL ENTREPRENEUR

OLE PROZAC

In June of 2001, my friend Kent asked me if I wanted to do some trail riding with him at a ranch in Wyoming. I agreed, and the next week we loaded up Kent's horse and picked up two other horses from his good friend, Harvey Yoakum. Harvey was larger than life. He talked with one of those deep, booming, West Texas voices that made one think they were listening to Paul Harvey or Rex Allen. People would listen intently to every word that came out of his mouth. Now living in Longmont Colorado, Harvey was a real old-time cowboy from Del City, Oklahoma. He had arranged the trip for Kent and me. We stayed at the Brush Creek Ranch in Saratoga, Wyoming. Brush Creek was situated in the heart of Wyoming's Platte River Valley, between the Sierra Madre Mountain range and the stunning Medicine Bow National Forest. We would go and enjoy a long weekend of trail riding, beer drinking, barn dancing, friendship, and . . . more beer drinking!

The Big Guy in the middle-Harvey Yoakum
his wife Carol to the left, Daughter to his right and me at
Brush Creek Ranch

I didn't want to take one of my Polo Ponies for fear of injuring a leg on the rocky trail rides, so Harvey brought an extra horse for me. The first day we saddled up, Harvey knew that I played Polo, had rodeoed, and was an experienced rider.

"What horse have you got for me today?" I asked.

"You will be on Ole Prozac, not everyone can ride him, but you won't have a problem, with all your rodeo and Polo experience." Now, I could understand the Polo experience, but began to question why he thought the rodeo experience would come in handy?

I climbed aboard Prozac without a problem, and we headed out. Ten minutes into the ride I could feel Prozac starting to bow-up like he wanted to buck. I became more than a little circumspect of Prozac and Harvey's grin when he assigned the horse to me.

"Harvey, does this horse buck?" I asked

"Nah, don't worry about it," He replied.

Later in the ride, Harvey admitted to me that no one had ever stayed aboard Prozac without eventually getting bucked off. *Oh, Great,* I thought, *how long do I have before it's my turn?*

The terrain was extremely rocky, and we were crossing rivers and streams with very slippery rocks. Consequently, it was a little unnerving given Prozac's proclivity to bucking. I was wishing that he hadn't told me. After a long day of riding through the mountains, we headed back to the ranch house.

Fifteen minutes from the ranch, we were greeted by one of the ranch hands on an ATV. He brought all of us a beer for the last leg of our trip.

I felt a little more relaxed on good ole Prozac now that I could see the ranch house 100 yards in front of us. Suddenly, I felt the big 1,500lb Buckskin beneath me tighten his muscles. He was ready to buck. I tried to calm him, but it was to no avail. Prozac threw himself in every direction. No matter what I did he wasn't giving up, and I knew I wasn't going to last much longer. If you know you are defeated, it is better to bail off on your own terms rather than being bucked off. I looked for a spot where I could bail off. Everywhere I looked the ground was consumed with jagged rocks. Nevertheless, I pulled the ripcord and landed hard on the rocky trail.

Other than some scrapes and bruises I got up and dusted myself off. After they saw that I was okay, Harvey and Kent couldn't control their laughter.

"I am so proud of you! You have been on Prozac for the past five hours, and no one has ever stayed on him for much more than ten minutes," Harvey chuckled.

"Kiger, you were 100-yards from breaking history," Kent affirmed.

That evening Harvey planned a special treat for all of us. We would have a cowboy campfire, cook steaks on the fire, and listen to country western music with a cowboy guitarist.

A Private Concert by Michael Martin Murphey
Compliments of Harvey Yoakum

Much to our surprise, the cowboy with a guitar was none

other than Michael Martin Murphey. There he was sitting around a campfire with an audience of twenty people, playing his Platinum-Certified songs *Wildfire,* and *Carolina Pines.* Along with a great selection of *Marty Robbins Country Ballads*, and much more. He played for about ninety minutes and stayed for a few hours just to chat with us. He was the real deal, a real cowboy, and a great entertainer. For someone like me, who loved old time Country and Western music, what a great thrill it was to meet and have a private concert from Michael Martin Murphey.

Harvey never told me how much it cost him, but I know he paid big money to have Murphey entertain us that night. I now forgave Harvey for destroying my ego by putting me on Prozac, knowing it was pretty much an absolute that I would get bucked off.

Chapter Seventeen

THE SERIAL ENTREPRENEUR

BOGOTA CAN BE SAFE

Later that fall, I headed to Argentina to play Polo and attend the Argentine Open. This would be my third trip to Argentina, and my second time playing Polo there. My friend Santiago Wulff, a Polo player from Argentina who I hired for some U.S. tournaments, arranged the trip. We played tournaments at La Cañada Polo Club and the San Diego Polo Club, (not to be confused with the one in Del Mar, California), the clubs were located about an hour from Buenos Aires and Palermo, where the Argentine Open is held. After a morning of playing Polo, we would race back to BA to catch the 40-goal Open games.

The Open tournament is played with the most elite, and top players in the world. There were only ten 10-goal Polo players in the world, and they were all there for the Open. Players are rated on a handicap system, from -2 (beginner) to 10-goals. It was astonishing to watch the best Polo players and teams compete.

After the Open match, everyone would gather below the stadium where there were numerous restaurants and bars. I saw a group of Americans smoking cigars, and went over to ask where I could purchase a cigar, they generously offered me one. After we had talked for a while, one of the guys suggested that I come to their club and play Polo on their fields. I thought this was a great offer and pursued the proposition.

"Where is your Club?" I innocently asked.

"Bogota Colombia," he told me matter-of-factly.

YIKES, this would be a good opportunity to be killed or kidnapped!

In 2002 Bogota was a hotbed of murder, corruption, drug trade, and kidnapping. The Medellin Cartel, under the strong-arm of Pablo Escobar Gaviria, had turned Bogota and Medellin into the world capital of the cocaine business. The situation became so dangerous that the U.S. consulate was closed for security concerns.

"Oh my God! Isn't it extremely dangerous in Bogota these days?" I asked my new Polo friend.

"You don't understand, let me explain . . . my friend Ken here is ex-CIA . . . the other two fellas are ex-Navy Seals. . . Joe was with the NSA and I was with the FBI." I listened with my mouth open. "When we meet your plane and pick you up on the tarmac, no one will f--k with you." I gave them a half-hearted nod of my head. "Furthermore, our Polo field is located on a United States Air Force Base. It couldn't be safer.

They had all been stationed in Bogota fighting the drug war and loved the country so much that after retiring, they decided to stay. We exchanged phone numbers, but I chickened out and never contacted them. . . and never played Polo in Bogota! First time I ever reneged on an invitation to play Polo.

Chapter Eighteen

THE SERIAL ENTREPRENEUR

GO WEST MY SON

I had survived the dot-com bust of the late nineties. But, with the advent of the wireless Network that was rapidly growing throughout North America; I could see that the need for long distance services and prepaid phone cards would soon become a thing of the past. KT&T's IVR business was still going strong with clients such as American Express, Conde Nast, Vanity Fair, Medtronic Corporation, and other Fortune 500 companies. But, powerful computers were getting smaller and cheaper by the day, and I could foresee many of these corporations taking their IVR services in-house.

I was licensed with the FCC in all fifty states. The telecom licenses were an expensive, arduous process to go through, and came with an extensive legal exercise. Fortunately, the licenses were a transferable, valuable asset to a potential buyer. So, in the spring of 2004, I sold KT&T.

The clothing store in Cherry Creek was doing okay, but not making me rich. If I had been sixty-five, it would have been a great retirement business, given that I lived two blocks from the store and could walk to work. The store was making sufficient money to cover its expenses, provide me an ample amount to pay my mortgage, with enough left over to have a little fun. However, that wasn't nearly good enough. I had a lot more fight and ambition left in me, and I was not ready to settle for a just-get-by existence.

My niece Kelly, and her husband Noah Burford, had developed a sizable mortgage company in Southern California. They needed a CFO for the company, and wanted me for the job. I accepted the position and made the decisions to close my Polo Gear store, find a buyer for the Polo Club, plus the seventeen additional acres in south Denver, and a buyer or renter for my condo in Cherry Creek. Surprisingly, I found a buyer fairly quickly for the Polo Club and a renter for the condo. One of the determining factors for my decision to take the job was it could afford me the opportunity to play Polo all-year-round in California. Additionally, I have always had an insatiable appetite to learn. *The Burford Group* would afford me the self-indulgence of learning the mechanics of the real estate and mortgage business.

I loaded up my eight horses and headed to the San Diego Polo Club. After dropping off the horses, I flew back to Denver to finish packing. One of the big supporters of my life was my oldest brother James. He flew to Denver to help me pack, and drive the moving truck. We headed west, and had our first stop for gas in a small town on the western edge of Colorado. After fueling, the truck failed to start and we were stranded in a town in the middle of nowhere, with no motel, no restaurant, and most importantly, no mechanic!

I called U-Haul and four hours later they sent out a repairman. The starter was shot and U-Haul could not bring another truck for two days. Even if they did we would have to unload and reload a 26-foot truck! The mechanic showed us how we could hit *the starter* with a hammer to make the truck start. He literally started the truck by beating it with a hammer! He showed me his arcane technique. That was good enough for me not to wait two days for a new truck. We happily headed down the road.

I pulled into a truck stop in Utah to gas up. Not wanting to take the chance of the truck not starting again, I left the truck running. Not a great safety measure. I pulled the gas nozzle from the pump, my brother was standing six feet from me. I turned the pump on and the gas immediately started gushing from the nozzle. Gas was flying everywhere. I drench my brother with gas, and it was spraying underneath the running truck and onto the hot exhaust pipes.

I couldn't believe how fast, and how much gas came out of the nozzle in a matter of seconds. The entire area was flooded with gas. I threw the nozzle down and ran to hit the emergency shut off. After the gas stopped flowing, I jumped in the truck and moved it away from the pool of gas it was sitting on.

My brother's eyes were burning from the gas I had sprayed on him. He went to the station to change his clothes, and wash out his eyes. The handle on the nozzle had been stuck in the ON position, so when I turned on the pump the fuel started flowing. We were panicked by what had just happened, and quickly got the hell out of there without getting gas. We drove to the next exit to stop for fuel. I shut off the truck, filled the tank, and utilized the mechanic's hammer technique to get us started again. I couldn't believe it worked! The smell of the gas fumes from our clothes and shoes were so asphyxiating, we had to drive the rest of the way to California with the windows down. We finally arrived in Newport Beach looking forward to a much-needed shower and sleep.

The next day after unloading the truck, I didn't even attempt to try to restart it, I just called U-Haul and I told them to come pick up their piece-of-shit vehicle. I can't believe how close I came to blowing up the truck, and possibly burning my brother alive.

Chapter Nineteen

THE SERIAL ENTREPRENEUR

SOME DOGS LOVE NUTS

The Newport Beach House that I purchased was one of the best homes I had ever owned. It was 3,200-sq. ft., three bedrooms, three baths and one-half bath that backed up to the Newport Country Club. The entire house that I grew up in would have fit into the kitchen.

What was the best part of the new home? It was ten minutes from my office, fifty minutes from the San Diego Polo Club, two hours from the El Dorado Polo Club in Palm Springs, and three hours from the Santa Barbara Polo Club. My longtime friend, Steve Crowder, managed my Polo. He arranged for a groom to take care of my horses, organized what teams I could play on, and hired the pros to play on my team. Steve was a great Polo player in his own right, but he was now retired from the sport due to too many concussions from Polo wrecks. It has been documented that Polo is the second most dangerous sport next to auto racing. Steve and I had something else in common; he rode bulls when he was in high school and college. But, Steve was a much better bull rider than I ever thought of being, he was one tough cowboy!

Steve was bringing up his son, Jason, to be great Polo player. He was already 4-goals at age seventeen. Jason would be a pro on my team for several tournaments at San Diego and Eldorado Polo. Like his father, he was fearless and tough as nails.

Jason had a half Pit Bull dog that was also tough. One afternoon, he and another Polo Pro were roughhousing in the aisle of the barn. As the wrestling continued, it got Jason's dog stirred up wanting to join in the action. Unfortunately, the dog's instincts kicked in and bit Jason right at the crotch. I watched him stand up and his white Polo jeans were covered in blood. When he took down his pants he was bleeding from the scrotum. Another player on our team Aston Wolf, loaded

Jason into his car to race him to the hospital.

Screaming down the street from the club they blew through a red light, causing a lady to t-bone them at the intersection. Now, two ambulances came, one to haul the lady off, and another for Jason.

Jason received eight stitches in his scrotum, and his sack was blown up bigger than a softball. The very next day he was set to play in the finals of a major Polo tournament. I thought there was no way he would be able to play. Steve was hard on the poor kid, he told Jason he had worked his butt off to get him contracted to play on that team and expected him to play!

"You're not sitting out due to some stupid roughhousing, and injuries that you caused and brought on yourself," Steve told his son.

I played my game in the morning and then went to watch the high goal tournament that Jason was supposed to play in. Not expecting to see him on the field, I was shocked to see that he was there. Jason is the kind of athlete that could jump on the back of a horse from the ground. However, on that day, he would need a step-stool to get himself on the horse. Unarguably, Jason played one of the greatest games he had ever played in his life. Winning the tournament, he stood up the entire game, never sitting in the saddle. I don't know how he managed; he must have been in terrible pain. Steve bred his son to be tough, and he was. All the tough-love paid off that day.

I played summer Polo in Del Mar and as soon as we finished, the horses were scheduled to take two months off. We could then head to Palm Springs to play the winter season. At the San Diego Polo Club, we played in the Gutierrez Memorial Cup; I will always remember it as one of the best tournaments I ever won. Each year the Gutierrez family made beautiful bronze trophies and came up from Mexico to present them to the winning team.

Fernando Gutierrez a former Polo player at San Diego was murdered gangland-style in 1997. The perpetrator pulled alongside Gutierrez's Mercedes and shot him five times in the face. Homicide Lt. Gerry Lipscomb leading the investigation for the San Diego Sheriff's Department had this to say:

"It appears that Gutierrez was targeted. The suspect—or suspects--appear to be very proficient at firing a weapon."

Although the murder was never solved, and the motive never determined, it was always speculated by Federal Agents that Fernando had business ties to the Tijuana drug cartel. That didn't make a lot of sense because Fernando's father was a very wealthy and respected businessman, and money wouldn't have been an issue for Fernando.

The Gutierrez family presenting trophies to the
Winning Gutierrez Memorial Cup Team
from rt: Clemente Zavaleta, Ashton Wolf,
Robert Kiger, and Robin Paicius

Like all sports, one should never give up. I learned this the hard way when we played in the finals of an 8-goal tournament in Palm Springs. After the beginning of the fifth chukker, we were ahead 11-2. With only two periods left to play, we had a commanding lead. I know that I started to relax and I am sure the rest of the team did as well. After the fifth chukker, we were leading 11-6. Still a comfortable lead with only one chukker and seven minutes left to play. At the end of the final chukker, we were tied 12-12. We were now confronted with sudden-death overtime. Our coach, Steve Crowder, was extremely livid. In the end, we lost in overtime 12-13. Hence you should never relax until the final bell is rung.

Although we lost that match, we had many successful wins at Del Mar and Eldorado. A Denver friend, who was also playing at Eldorado, asked me how I made it to the finals of so many tournaments. I said the answer is easy, "Pick the right pros to play on your team." The best example was our *Holiday Cup*, 8-goal team. With three pros, Jason Crowder, Joseph Stuart, and Ashton Wolf, we were unstoppable. The best part? I stole Joseph from the Carnation Farms Polo team.

He was the fifth generation Grandson of Eldridge Amos Stuart, founder of the Carnation Milk Company in 1899, and the creator of Carnation Evaporated Milk. Later in 1984,

Carnation got sold to Nestles for $3 billion. Joseph's mother Dina, also a Polo player, was the sponsor of the Carnation Team. Obliviously, she wasn't too happy when she learned that Joseph would be playing on our team and against the Carnation team. In the finals, we won handily 8-5 against Carnation. Joseph scored 5 of our 8 goals, proving my point, it's all about the pros you hire. It was a bit of a slap in the face to Dina, but she was a great sport about it.

Holiday Cup Team
From Lf: Joseph Stuart, Robert Kiger,
Ashton Wolf, and Jason Crowder

Chapter Twenty

THE SERIAL ENTREPRENEUR

THE MORTGAGE BUST

After three years at the mortgage company, I took ownership of the firm under a new name, Polo Financial. We had built a great firm with sixty branch offices, and two hundred and fifty approved lenders on our lender list. We had major lenders like Wells Fargo, Indy Mac, Citi Bank, Bank of America, etc. I had survived many national economic downturns in the past – like real estate, oil & gas, the S&L crash of the late eighties, and the dot-com bust in the early 2000's. However, I had never seen a downturn like the mortgage-banking crisis of 2008.

During previous business regressions, I saw them coming, slowly but surely, as the downturn raised its ugly head. The mortgage, banking, and real estate bust was a totally different animal. In February 2008 it was like a fire hose had got turned on full blast, and by April the spigot was shut off hard. Within thirty days, our list of two hundred and fifty lenders was down to forty. The lenders wrote letters telling us to shut off the loan pipeline; they were getting out of the mortgage business. Countrywide, a major lender in Orange County, was closing its doors leaving hundreds of people without jobs. In sixty days our seventy branch offices were down to four. We had plenty of mortgage applications, but nowhere to place the loans. It came time for me to reinvent myself once again.

My home in Newport Beach got appraised for $1.7 million in 2007, but by May of 2008, the market was in the dumpster. I sold the property for $875,000. After the sale, I headed to Dallas, Texas to do some real estate consulting for an old friend Christopher Henry.

He had a very interesting company. Christopher was buying run-down homes in downtown Dallas and the sounding areas for incredibly low prices. Christopher would purchase two and three bedroom homes for $25,000 to $50,000. Then fix them up, putting $5,000 - $7,000 in each, and then would turn them into Section 8 rentals. Ingenious, having the government guarantee him 75% of the monthly rental, while the other 25% was the responsibility of the renter.

One of the renters called to inform us that her ex-boyfriend beat her up and had broken the front window. When we arrived at the property, the Dallas police were already on the scene. An officer informed her that she needed to take out a restraining order on the guy. He further suggested she should get a gun, and if her boyfriend came on the property again, she should shoot him. Now that's some real cowboy advice. I don't think that advice was in the police officers handbook, do you?

Chapter Twenty-One

THE SERIAL ENTREPRENEUR

ELEGANTE' POLO

Dallas is a great city, and unlike California, the people are incredibly friendly. Going to a Dallas restaurant by yourself is quite an experience. I found that by the time I was ready to leave, I had probably made fifteen new friends. I wanted to stay and enjoy the hospitality that the city extended, but my consulting gig in Dallas was unfortunately up, and the time had come to a head back to Florida.

Another Polo playing friend of mine, Ron Allen was the promotional and advertising director for the Villages Polo Club outside of Ocala, Florida. I met him while playing Polo at the Denver Polo Club. He had been the local ABC affiliate weather anchor in Denver. He asked me to come to Ocala for six months to help them build-out a Polo store in the stadium of the Polo club.

I accepted the offer, and soon I had organized and built a beautiful store for them. When my six months were up, *The Villages'* senior management asked me to stay on to be the assistant manager of the club, I agreed. Then without warning, two weeks later, they fired my pal Ron Allen who had been there almost from the inception of the club in 1999. I was shocked, and this wasn't acceptable to me.

How could I stay when Ron had gotten me the job, and now he was out, and I got in? As much as I adored the owners of *The Villages* and the amazing empire they had built, I resigned my position. I couldn't imagine staying on and doing that to my friend Ron Allen.

Reinvention time again! I wanted to open a clothing store in Palm Beach. I asked Ron if he would like to come with me to Palm Beach to help run the store. He agreed, and we set out to find a space. We either needed to be close to the International Polo Club in Wellington, or be on Worth Avenue on Palm Beach Island. We envisioned that the store would be a high-end men and women's clothing and we needed to be where the money flowed.

We looked at various venues and finally settled on a spot in Wellington, one mile from the International Polo Club, and the Palm Beach Polo Club. We put in long days, sometimes eighteen to twenty hours. Two months later, the build-out was completed in record time, and we opened the doors of Elegante` Polo in early 2010. Once again, I applied the same concept that I had done in Denver. When entering the store, I wanted customers to feel like they had just arrived at a Ralph Lauren Boutique. Many patrons commented that the store looked just like the Ralph Lauren store in Chicago.

That was a huge compliment for me, as this was exactly the look I wanted to project. In fact, we had Ralph Lauren clothing, accessories, and *Ralph Lauren Home* in the store. Additionally, we had *Vicomte A* from Paris, *La Martina* and *Etiqueta Negra* both from Argentina, and many other unique brands from around the globe.

Elegante` Polo could be much likened to the early days of Neiman Marcus. In the 1980's patrons of Neiman's could find incredibly unique one-of-a-kind items that one would never see anywhere else. Nowadays when everything is so mass produced in China, walking into at Nieman Marcus is much the same experience as shopping at Saks, Bloomingdale's or Macy's. I wanted to bring back the unique shopping experience Neiman's had once been famous for, like beautiful dresses for women, men's sports clothing and blazers to wear at Sunday Polo or a big night out on the town. Women didn't have to fear being seen in the same dress, as we only purchased one size run for any given item. I was very fortunate to be able to obtain a contract with Ralph Lauren since they never allowed their product into independent boutiques.

Elegante' Polo Flagship Store

Elegante Polo sponsored many Polo teams and tournaments, which I played in. We also sponsored women's teams for Miami Beach Polo and Chicago Beach Polo. Elegante` orchestrated several fashion shows utilizing many of my beautiful Polo and Equestrian friends that weren't professional models, but with a little coaching, they looked like they had modeled their entire life. Fulfilling my love for fashion, and my passion for Polo, this was one of the greatest periods of my career.

I hired Mauricio Devrient as my Polo pro to play on the Elegante` Polo Team. We were playing a tournament at Palm Beach Polo, and during the first chukker, an opposing player and I were racing towards the goal. We were going for the ball that was lying in front of the goal post, both riding at a sharp angle toward each other. Our horses bumped way too hard causing them to spook at the goal posts that suddenly appeared right in their path and in front of their eyes.

Both horses ducked out from under us and the opposing player and I went slamming to the ground. I didn't get up. Instantly knowing something was terribly wrong, my dog Bella, who always sat quietly on the sidelines during our matches, immediately came racing to me as I lay unconscious on the ground.

Bella, The Elegante` Polo Dog

Mauricio stood over me screaming, "Kiger wake up, Kiger wake up." After about three minutes I finally came to. As I sat on the back of the ambulance I kept telling the EMT's that I was okay and was ready to continue playing. Mauricio and the EMTs were insistent that I go to the Emergency Room to be checked out. I unwillingly agreed, and my groom played out the rest of the game for me.

After spending about three hours in the ER, Mauricio's

girlfriend, Melissa, picked me up and took me to the Polo Club, where my horses were stabled and Bella was waiting. There just happened to be a game starting at the club and they needed another player. I hadn't gotten to play much Polo that day, and against the doctor's advice, I quickly instructed my groom to tack up my first horse. Five minutes later I mounted my horse and then five others as I played all six chukkers. After the game, Mauricio commented, "You just played the best Polo match I have ever seen you play. Maybe you should get knocked out more often," he laughed.

In 2012 I hired Omar Sosa and his son Matias to be the pros for the Elegante` Polo Team. Omar, now rated 4-goals had been a former 10-goal player from Brazil. His son was rated 2-goals. Omar had amazing abilities stemming from his 10-goal experiences that he had never forgotten. He still had incredible speed and accuracy of his shots sixty-yards out from the goal. Not to disparage any of the other incredible pros that I had in California, Florida, Denver, or anywhere else, but I won more tournaments with Omar and his son in two years than I had with any other set of pros.

Victors of the Metropolitan Cup – Elegante` Polo teammates
Robert Kiger, Mason Primm (subbing for the injured Matias Sosa)
Shamir Quareshi, and Omar Sosa.

In 2015, our lease for Elegante` Polo was up for renewal. Prudential was the management company for our shopping center. Here is an example of how stupid large real estate management companies can be. They wanted me to sign another five-year lease with a substantial increase in monthly rent. I told them that I would sign a new five-year deal, but I wanted a decrease in monthly rent. They refused my offer.

"Okay, how about letting me go month-to-month at the same rate, and if you get a renter that will sign a five-year lease for an increased price, give me sixty days and I will move out," I proposed. Again, their response was "NO". What stupidity! As it turned out, the space sat empty for eighteen months after I closed Elegante` Polo.

After closing the main store location, it didn't make any sense for me to keep open my second location, which had been established inside The Palm Beach Polo and Country Club. So, after liquidating the inventory of both stores, it was time to reinvent once again!

Chapter Twenty-Two

THE SERIAL ENTREPRENEUR

THE BIRTH OF CITIZENS

We all know the saying: *To be successful you have to do what you love.* Well, I asked myself, "What did I love that I hadn't already done?" The answer came to mind immediately, *POLITICS!*

Over the last eight years, I had become frustrated sitting around complaining about President Barrack Obama. I believed that he was destroying our country. It was time for me to stop whining and try to do something about it. But what could I do? After giving it a lot of thought, I wasn't coming up with any big ideas. Then, days later, driving down the road with my Denver pal, Chuck Correll, the idea hit me like a ton of bricks.

"I could start a Political Action Committee to raise money to elect a Republican President," I told Chuck. I quickly handed over my phone and credit card.

"Before I forget the epiphany I just had, call Go-Daddy and see if *Citizens for Restoring USA* domain is available. If so, reserve and buy that name." The domain was available, and *Citizens for Restoring USA* gave birth.

When I returned to my office the next day, I completed all the necessary paperwork and filed the *Political Action Committee* with the Federal Election Commission. Responding very quickly, my *PAC* was approved by the FEC on April 15th, 2015.

At the time of the inception, I didn't support a specific candidate or take on a specific issue, but it was my goal to support a Republican Presidential candidate who could turn this country around. Many Republican candidates had already announced intentions to run for the 2016 Presidential Election. None of which excited me. They were part of the old beltway establishment crowd that would continue to be more of the same. I didn't think any of these men, and one woman would be a part of a solution to change America from the economic stagnation that we were facing.

On December 16th, 2014, Jeb Bush established a PAC for a possible run. Although I loved the Bush family, I thought the country clearly had enough of the name Bush. In January 2016, Chris Christie formed a PAC and intended to run. I liked Governor Christie's straight talk and tough guy, no-nonsense approach to the issues, but thought the *Bridgegate* scandal would plague him to defeat. Also, throwing in their hat to the Presidential ring was Dr. Ben Carson, and Senator Lindsey Graham. I didn't think that either of those two candidates stood a chance of beating Hillary Clinton.

Then Donald Trump announced he had formed an exploratory committee on March 23rd, 2015. The light went off! I instantly knew that I had found my dream candidate. Most speculated he would not run and this was just another publicity stunt to further improve ratings for the upcoming season of Celebrity Apprentice. But, Trump had made a statement two years' prior that if the country was still in bad shape, he would run. I couldn't imagine our country being in worst shape, so I was convinced he would enter the race.

Citizens for Restoring USA declared Donald Trump as the candidate we would support.

The *PAC* began receiving donor support. Not surprising, the first donation came from a friend of mine. To my shock, the second contribution was from a gentleman living in San Francisco, California. My curiosity was aroused, *Why the hell did a San Franciscan send $100?* I thought. I had to discover his motivation.

I called him to say "thank you" for the support, and asked why he was backing the Trump candidacy? He told me that he was a fifty-five-year-old college graduate, who had been a Democrat all his life. He had voted Jimmy Carter, Walter Mondale, Michael Dukakis, Bill Clinton, Al Gore, and Barack Obama twice. "I am sickened by the direction of this country," he retorted adamantly. "Obama has ruined our great nation."

I knew right then, and thought to myself: *There will be a vast silent majority during this election who will emerge to elect Donald Trump.*

Chapter Twenty-Three

THE SERIAL ENTREPRENEUR

FAKE NEWS

The Washington Post discovered our filing with the FEC, and on May 22nd they called me for an interview. They asked Trump if he knew about the *PAC* or knew Robert Kiger? He had heard about the *PAC*, but didn't know me, but was pleased to have my support. Although the Washington Post story was fair and factual, I soon realized in subsequent interviews that the liberal Press would mangle the facts, and spin any story to fit their agenda. No matter how polite and gracious they were on the phone, they were not to be trusted, and they were not your friend. Interviews with Politico, the Palm Beach Post, and others evinced exactly that.

The PB Post wrote nothing about the issues or policy we discussed. They spewed out that we were just wealthy equestrians who didn't have anything better to do with our money and had no concept of what a hard life was all about. I guess they hadn't seen the shack that I got born and raised in.

The headline read,

Donald Trump: The President for disenfranchised equestrians? The article described Donald Trump as, *A gaudy billionaire in the midst of another make-believe campaign.*

The Post jabbed at downtrodden equestrians saying,

Nobody's been willing to bring attention to the dire needs of those people who jet around the world with a bunch of pampered ponies to play what's commonly called "The Sport of Kings." But their voices in the upcoming election need to be heard. And it will be so refreshing to have some Spanish- speaking immigrants that Republicans can embrace.

That kind of trash talk became my first experience with "Fake News."

Chapter Twenty-Four

THE SERIAL ENTREPRENEUR

A DAY TO REMEMBER

Trump was set to make a speech from Trump Tower on June 16th. He would announce his decision whether he was running or not. At 6 p.m. on June 15th, I received a call from Fox News, they wanted to schedule an interview with me right after the Trump's speech in New York. I agreed. Holy crap! My *PAC* had made *The Big Time*. The Fox News Limo picked me up at my Polo farm in Wellington and we drove to the studio that Fox and CCN use in Boynton Beach, about thirty minutes from Palm Beach.

Neil Cavuto was the interviewer, and he tried to beat me up over Trump's comment regarding illegals coming from Mexico. Trump said in his announcement speech from Trump Tower, ***Mexico is not sending their best. There' not*** *sending you. They're sending people that have lots of problems, and they're bringing those problems with them. They're bringing drugs. They're bringing crime. They're rapists. And some, I assume, are good people.*

Trying to get off the subject of whether Trump's statement was impolitic, I told Neil that it was imperative that the United States secure the southern border. All Presidents, Republican and Democrat dating back to Ronald Reagan had promised to secure the Border, and all of them had failed! We could no longer afford to worry about hurting people's feelings; America must secure its Southern border.

Neil didn't think that Trump could win. I told him that Trump would win the Republican nomination over the field of seventeen, and would become the next President of the United States. He pretty much laughed at me, as Trump was polling at two percent at the time. So I bet him a dinner that Trump would win. He agreed, but stipulated that if he won, I would buy dinner at Del Frisco's in New York and if I won, he would take me to Wendy's.

Robert Kiger on the Fox Business News Set with Neil Cavuto

I must have done a decent job on Fox because the next morning I got a call from CNN to join Carol Costello the host of American Newsroom. Again, the subject was Trump's tone, and language. "A lot of people don't like the words he is choosing to describe things, specifically immigration," she said. I was ready with my answer.

"People are tired of political correctness in this country. They need a game changer and someone who will get in people's faces," I took a breath and continued. "The miasma of his remarks during his announcement speech got trumped-up and obfuscated by the media. They don't want Trump to be the nominee because they know he will beat Hillary Clinton!" I don't think she liked my media comment, but I continued to receive more invitations from CNN.

Chapter Twenty-Five

THE SERIAL ENTREPRENEUR

TRUMP'S NOT SO PC

On July 18th, during a campaign stop in Iowa, Trump commented that John McCain, *Was not a war hero. He's a war hero because he was captured. I like people who weren't captured.* This set off another firestorm with the Mainstream Media. I got the call and was booked on CNN and Fox the following day. Trump's McCain comment was the focus. I shared this statement, "You may not like the way Donald Trump speaks, but if it rips the scab off a wound and brings to light how terribly the Veterans have been treated in this country, then so be it. We have got to cowboy-up, political correctness is completely and totally out of control in this country."

I seemed to be the only one in the world who thought

Trump would win. When Trump made a comment that the media didn't like, I had suddenly become the to-go-guy. Unfortunately, for Mr. Trump, they didn't like much of whatever he would say. But, it was fortunate for me, as my media exposure continued to grow.

During the first presidential debate Fox News host Megyn Kelly came out firing with her first question to Trump, *"Mr. Trump, one of the things people love about you is you speak your mind and you don't use a politician's filter. However, that is not without its downsides, in particular, when it comes to women. You've called women you don't like, fat pigs, dogs, slobs, and disgusting animals."*

Fox News host, Chris Wallace, was also on the moderating panel firing questions at Trump. All the questions were personal and disparaging with regard to Trump's past. I thought to myself. *Where the hell were the policy questions for candidate Trump.* Those questions were not to be found! It was evident that the Fox News moderators had it in for Trump. Throwing softball questions to the rest of the GOP field, while personally attacking Trump.

The next day the media outrage continued, CNN's Don Lemon asked Trump about Megyn Kelly's first question. Trump responded, "You could see there was blood coming out of her eyes, blood coming out of her wherever." Another

whirlwind media frenzy hit the networks and the print media.

Once again, I was asked to appear on Fox and CNN. Surely by now, they thought that my support would have diminished. . . How could anyone defend such an abrasive comment? Contrary to their popular belief, my support had not wavered. I turned the question into a hit on the moderators and their attempt to dish out "gotcha" questions for Trump. I thought they lost a little credibility. The debate seemed to be more about the panelists asking the questions and their attempt to embarrass Donald

Trump. They gave easy questions to the rest of the candidates, like asking Jeb Bush about Common Core. Really? An issue that Jeb had been preaching and studying for years! Why not ask him if the sun rises in the East?

I disparaged the Fox News Debate Moderators on their own channel and had broken an unwritten cardinal rule. I suspicioned that is why I was never asked to appear on Fox News again. Apparently, they couldn't handle a little honest criticism. But, I did continue to be a frequent guest on CNN prior to the election.

One morning in September 2015, I went to my office to work on another pro-Trump video. When I turned on my computer I was shocked, as there were no files on the PC! I wasn't concerned because I had another separate computer dedicated to completely backing up and mirroring my main PC. I also had an external hard drive backing up both, as well as thumbnail drives backing up important banking files, financial data, and reports to the Federal Election Commission. But, I soon discovered all of the data was lost. I couldn't retrieve any documents from any of my multiple sources. Now, it was time for me to freak out!

I rushed my PC's and the external drive to a computer security expert whom I was friends with. We did not have any power outages or lightning storms that might have caused my PC's malfunction. The expert told me that he had never seen anything like it. All files and root programs were wiped completely clean on both computers, the external backup drive, and the thumbnail drives. This was the work of Black-hat professionals.

I felt that in light of the hacking scandals that surfaced surrounding the 2016 Election, and given that I was the only *PAC* supporting Trump at that time, I speculated that it was the work of the Democratic National Committee or a Russian hacker.

Chapter Twenty-Six

THE SERIAL ENTREPRENEUR

THEY ALL OWE ME DINNER

In October, I attended a political conference in Los Angeles. Many political media moguls were there including Newt Gingrich, Ann Coulter, Michele Bachmann, etc. I was there to be interviewed by the liberal commentator of the "Young Turks", Cenk Uygur. During the interview, I presented Uygur with a "Trump 2016" ball cap and bet him a steak dinner at Mastro's in LA if Trump won the Presidency. Uygur became one in a long list of news commentators that lost bets, and would owe me dinner after the election. Unfortunately, none of them have paid up. It was amazing the common ground that this ultra-liberal and I uncovered. Uygur agreed with me that Obama had done nothing for Black America. The unemployment rate during the Obama

Administration was off the charts, and racial relations in America was at the lowest point since 1965. Uygur was much more pleasant to me then he was to Ann Coulter. As always, Ann held her own in the room filled with Young Turk's supporters, but I thought that it was wise she had her bodyguard close at hand.

Two months prior, Ann Coulter was on Bill Maher's show and she was asked, "Of all seventeen Republican Nominees running for president, which one has the best chance of winning?" her response, "Donald Trump!" She drew as much laughter from the crowd as I did on Fox and CNN when I declared that he would win.

During a one-on-one discussion panel with Ann at the LA convention, I told her that on the day Trump announced his Presidential run, I told Fox News that Donald Trump would be the next Republican nominee and the next President of the United States and I had dinner bets with commentators from Fox News, CNN, the Young Turks and others.

"Wait a minute, you said this on air that Donald Trump would be President?" she asked shocked.

"Yes, I most certainly did!"

"Do you give investment advice, because I am buying whatever you suggest! You need to frame your Trump declaration!" she laughed.

In later interviews, I added the prediction that Trump would win in a Reaganesque landslide. Based on the eventual Electoral Map, I was correct.

During that same LA convention, I was sitting at a table with Michael Steele, MSNBC commentator and prior head of the Republican National Committee, an executive from Newsmax, some other RNC officials, and other media bigwigs. I told them of my predictions regarding Trump. Again the unanimous response was, "Kiger you're crazy, he doesn't stand a chance."

Most notable was Alex Castellanos, who thought Trump was a clown and no way could win. His criticism was intense; he even considered creating a "Stop Trump" movement, calling for a "negative ad blitz" against Trump. In June 2016, after Trump had won the Republican nomination, Castellanos became the spokesperson and head strategist for the "Rebuilding America Now" PAC, which was a pro-Trump PAC funded by my Polo playing friend and California real estate mogul Tom Barrick.

The hypocrisy of Castellanos running the pro-Trump PAC was unimaginable.

It never ceases to amaze me how money can change the opinion of the DC establishment.

Chapter Twenty-Seven

THE SERIAL ENTREPRENEUR

HERE COME THE DEATH THREATS

In December 2015, Trump held a rally in Birmingham, Alabama. A man holding a *Black Lives Matter* sign started to scream in the middle of Trump's speech.

"Black Lives Matter, Black Lives Matter!"

Security jumped into action, and as they were ushering him out, the man threw himself on the ground, dramatically complaining of being roughed up by security. The commotion didn't faze Trump at all, he just leaned into the microphone calling for security, "Get him out! Get him out of here!"

On CNN the next day Carol Castello asked for my comment. I said, "Well I hadn't seen the video, but..." Seemingly annoyed, she quickly interrupted and fired back, "I just played the video on air." I didn't want to embarrass her by telling the viewers that there wasn't a monitor in the studio that would allow me to view what she was playing on air. I responded accordingly.

"I wouldn't be surprised if he got roughed up a bit. If I walked into a black church and started screaming, *White Lives Matter*, I would and quite frankly, should be thrown out.

"Do you really think that you would be beaten up in a black church? Castello asked.

"Yes, I might be roughed up a bit in the process," I shot back at her. "The *Black Lives Matter* movement had no business being there in the first place, they were only there to disrupt. If they really cared about black lives, they would pick up their banners and go to the south side of Chicago where hundreds of black lives are being slaughtered on a monthly basis" I reiterated.

Now I had become the subject of the media storm; labeled a bigot, racist, and a homophobe. The headlines read:

Trump supporter and bigot Robert Kiger: *I'd get beat up at a black church.*

Head of Trump Super PAC accidentally admits Donald's rallies are only for white people...

*Robert Kiger on the CNN News Set
with Carol Castello*

The social media attacks were beyond belief. And then came the death threats. One even went so far as to put a bounty on my head for $25,000 and posted it on Facebook. It didn't bother me, except for pissing me off that the bounty was only $25k, wasn't my life was worth at least $50,000?

I always loved to work with my hands, building-out stores, remodeling not only my homes, but also homes of others. John and Connie Wise, my friends from *The Villages Polo Club* days, called me to do some painting at their beautiful home in the Palm Beach Polo Club. This was a great diversion from my work on the campaign, so I agreed to do the job. One day I was up on a ladder fifteen feet in the air with my hands full of paint; the phone rang, and it was Wolf Blitzer's producer at CNN. They wanted me to appear with Wolf on the "Situation Room" show in ninety minutes. With paint on me from head to toe, I had to turn the invite down. From that point forward I was known as *The Celebrity Painter.*

I was predominately self-funding my *PAC,* and during the campaign, I created and produced more than one hundred videos and ads in support of Donald Trump. My National Director, Brooks Thornhill and I, worked hard to build more than forty thousand devoted followers on Facebook.

In some instances, because of the multitude of *Shares*, a video that we posted on the *Citizens Facebook* page would reach more than four million potential voters. The power of social media was incredible.

Twenty-eight days from Election Day, I released a video entitled, "Trump's Landslide." At that time, most polls had

Hillary Clinton leading Donald Trump by double digits. On October 10th, the day I released the video, an NBC/Wall Street Journal poll had Clinton with a fourteen percentage-point lead over Trump. My *"Landslide"* video reminded viewers not to be dismayed or trust the polls; on October 26th 1980, Ronald Reagan trailed President Jimmy Carter 39% to 47%. A Gallop poll had Reagan losing the election by eight percentage points twelve days before the election. Of course, Reagan went on to win the election by ten points. I had said fourteen months ago on CNN that Trump would win in a landslide, and at that point, I still adamantly believed it.

Chapter Twenty-Eight

THE SERIAL ENTREPRENEUR

ELECTION NIGHT

On election night, I had dinner with a few friends at Mar-a-Lago and watched the election results come in. After dinner, we went into one of the big ballrooms equipped with multiple TV's, and free-flowing champagne. The commentators were still convinced that Clinton would win. By 10:39 p.m., their enthusiasm started to wane a bit when Trump won the key battleground state of Ohio. At 10:53 p.m., the cheers in the room were enormous when Florida and its twenty-nine electoral votes were called for Trump. But, the media continued to cheerlead for Clinton, exhibiting pathways of how she could beat Trump. Maybe she could win Wisconsin, Michigan, Pennsylvania, and North Carolina?

Fifteen minutes later the media hope for a Clinton win

began to fade as the race in North Carolina got called for Trump. Then Trump picked up Utah and Iowa. At 1:35 a.m., Trump clinched Pennsylvania, he now had 264 electoral votes of the 270 needed to win. If Trump could win Michigan, Wisconsin or Arizona, he would be the 45th President of the United States. I declared to my friend Derek Smith, "Let's go! Trump has this in the bag, and I've had enough Mar-a-Lago champagne!"

I watched the balance of the results from my Palm Beach cottage. At 2.07 a.m., John Podesta was still refusing to concede defeat, even though there was no path for a Clinton win. Per to Corey Lewandowski, who was with Donald Trump that night on the 66th floor of Trump Tower, the Associated Press called Kellyanne Conway at 2:20 a.m., to inform the campaign they were calling it. She wanted to know which state they were calling for Trump? The AP editor said, "We are not calling a state, we are calling the race!" At 2:30 a.m., Trump won Wisconsin, giving him more than the needed, 270 electoral votes. Five minutes later, at 2:35 a.m., all of the networks were calling the race; Donald J. Trump was now President-elect Trump. I went to sleep at 4:30 a.m. knowing we now had a President who was going to *"Make America Great Again."*

Chapter Twenty-Nine

THE SERIAL ENTREPRENEUR

LIFE AFTER TRUMP

I am still waiting for the call from the White House to work for President Trump. He needs more individuals like myself who will support his agenda and help him *Make America Great Again.* I can't figure out why the Trump administration permits themselves to be continually plagued with the Obama-era holdouts. Isn't it obvious that they don't support our President?

After the election, I felt like a kid on Christmas morning. I was elated that we had the incredible gift of a President-elect Trump, but sad that the anticipation of opening the gift was now over. I was looking for the next Mentor and my next project. *Citizens For Restoring USA* would continue to work hard to support conservative Republicans, but I needed to do more. Then out-of-the-blue, I received a call from Carla

Spalding. She told me that she was running for a U.S. Congressional seat in Florida's 23rd District. Carla wanted me to be the Campaign and Finance Chairman. I knew that Florida's 23rd District was held by Debbie Wasserman Schultz. I wanted nothing more than to get Wasserman Schultz voted out of office. Carla had the perfect pedigree to beat Debbie; a Navy Veteran, a registered nurse with a Master's Degree, she worked at the Veteran VA Hospital for six years, she was a single mother, and she is a black woman. If anyone could oust Schultz in this predominately Democratic stronghold, it was Carla. Furthermore, if there was ever a perfect time to remove Schultz, 2018 was the year.

While Debbie was the Chairman of the Democratic National Committee, WikiLeaks released emails providing evidence that she was stacking the deck against Hillary Clinton's Primary challenger, Bernie Sanders. The Democrat and Republican National Committees are supposed to remain neutral during Primary elections. She had clearly broken the rules. Now embroiled in controversy, she was nowhere to be found during the 2016 Democratic Convention, and her scheduled speech had been canceled. Schultz stepped down as Chairwoman just after the Convention.

Many Democratic officials just wanted Schultz to go

away. She got booed at a Florida Delegation breakfast speech, with attendees shouting "shame!" Schultz had another big problem; an *IT* staffer under her employ was under federal investigation for equipment and data scam at the U.S. House of Representatives. Other House Representatives used Imram Awan, and four of his relatives plus another friend for various *IT* matters. They were all under investigation. The other House Members immediately fired Imram and his *IT* group. Schultz refused to fire them vociferating citing that it was just Republican Muslim Bigotry. She finally fired him the day after he was arrested by federal authorities. This was a full six months after the scandal broke and other House Members had already canned Imram.

With Schultz being such a close ally of Hillary, now I had the opportunity beat a Clinton cohort, so I accepted the position with Spalding. Carla arranged for me to meet with Stanley Tate. I was excited to have the meeting because this man was a real *Republican King Maker*.

When I arrived at Tate's office in North Miami, I was astonished. Literally, from floor to ceiling, every hallway and the conference room was lined with hundreds of eight by ten photos of Tate and every President, Senator, Congressman, and World Leader that had been in office for the last sixty years. Tate, now eighty-nine-years-old, remains as bright, sharp, and articulate as you can imagine. I asked him if he worked every day. Dumb question! He is in his office every morning at 8 a.m., and usually doesn't leave before 6 p.m.

Mr. Tate worked in the White House under two Presidents; H.W. Bush and Bill Clinton as the Chairman of the Resolution Trust Corporation. The RTC was the agency that managed and liquidated banks. Tate was credited with saving the US banking system during the S&L crisis in the late eighties and early nineties. As I talked with Mr. Tate, it was clear that his most cherished accomplishment was the establishment of the Prepaid College Tuition Program. The program is designed to help low-income families pay tuition over an eighteen-year in stallment plan, and it's still going strong. The program is attributable to hundreds of thousands of students receiving a four-year degree.

I listened intently to Mr. Tate as he told me story after story of his incredible life's work. My favorite Tate exploit was his purchase of Studio 54 in New York City. He purchased the nightclub from the IRS after they had seized the property from the previous owners who had gone to prison for tax evasion. He told me that he had acquired the property for pennies on the dollar. Two years after he reopened Studio 54, he sold the club for $10 million. The buyer paid $5 million down and got to pay the remaining $5 million in twelve months. The buyer defaulted on the second payment, and Tate took the club back. Four years later he sold it once again, this time for $20 million.

I told Mr. Tate that one of my favorite leaders was Israel's Prime Minister, Benjamin Netanyahu. I thought that his speech to the Joint Session of Congress was remarkable, and in my opinion, John Boehner arranging for Netanyahu to address the Joint Session was the only notable accomplishment achieved by the House Speaker.

"Funny you mention that, I am leaving to be with Bibi in a few days," Tate said.

Then he told me he was leaving at the end of the week on a supersonic jet which was being developed for the military by one of his friends.

"There are only two of these planes in existence, they only seat five people including the pilots, and fly at 76,000 feet. Instead of taking fourteen hours to get to Tel Aviv, I will be there in six and a half hours," Tate proclaimed. But that wasn't the best part of the story; Tate was scheduled to address the Knesset, the Israeli equivalent of our Congress.

Robert Kiger with the "King Maker" Stanley G. Tate

He and Netanyahu are very close friends, and Stanley would

stay at Beit Aghion, the private residence of Netanyahu. After m eeting with Tate, I knew that I had found my next great mentor.

Tate has been married to his lovely wife, Joni, for sixty-nine years. Maybe he could teach me something about holding on to a good woman.

Robert Kiger driving in the Presidential Motorcade

I did receive a call from the White House, but it was not exactly the call I'm waiting for. The caller was from the White House Advance Team. Ken Baker, a friend of mine had given them my name to be a driver in the Presidential Motorcade when President Trump comes to Florida.

Although I wasn't headed to DC, it has become the greatest honor of my life! It is extremely exciting to be a part of the advance team and drive support for President Trump. I am awed by the army of Secret Service agents and Palm Beach Sheriff Tactical Unit officers that it takes to move the President and the forty-car motorcade. Just to be on the inside and watch the logistics that these dedicated men and women go through is jaw-dropping.

Many people have suggested and encouraged me to write this book. I procrastinated and tried to talk myself out of it for all the usual insecure reasons:

Maybe no one will read it!
Who cares what I think?
What if nobody buys it?

Then I remembered what Gandhi once said:

"*Whatever you do in life will be insignificant, but it is very important that you do it.*"

The End

ABOUT THE AUTHOR

Robert Kiger is a frequent guest commentator on Fox News, CNN, and other national media outlets. He has an extensive background in management and sales, his overall experience exceeds twenty-five years. This includes twenty years of Executive Officer experience with various private and publicly held institutions.

His sales and management skills have been applied to administering equine and other purebred livestock operations, juxtaposed with insurance, finance and lending operations, telecommunications, and marketing.

Kiger has also been instrumental in developing various plans and models taking companies from a financial deficit to profitability in a short period. He has evaluated existing operations as well as developed prudent action plans for the successful reorganization of departments to increase sales and reducing operating costs while improving efficiency.

 Most recently, after seeing what had been happening to the country under the Obama Administration, Mr. Kiger founded the *Citizens for Restoring USA*. He organized the *PAC* in April 2015 and devoted its support to elect conservative leaders who are dedicated to *Making America Great Again. Citizens for Restoring USA* is fueled by the truth and strength of thousands of grass-roots activist's intents on breaking through the resistance of Washington's powerful elites. *Citizens for Restoring USA* was the first *PAC to* support Donald Trump's 2016 Presidential Candidacy.

Sharing conservative ideas and solutions for Job Creation, Limited Government, Veteran Care, Border Security, Repeal and Replacement of Obamacare, and rebuilding our Military back to pre-Obama levels, are the issues that are at the forefront of the PAC's ideology.

From Poverty to Polo to Politics

A Life Leading to Trump

Made in the USA
Middletown, DE
04 June 2021

40527614R00116